THROUGH MY HAT

by

Leonard Barras

These articles were first published in The Sunday Sun,
Newcastle upon Tyne, 1949–56.

Published by IRON Press, 5 Marden Terrace, Cullercoats,
North Shields, Tyne & Wear NE30 4PD. Tel: 091–253 1901.

Printed by Peterson Printers, South Shields.

Typeset by Roger Booth Associates in Stone Serif 9 point.

ISBN 0 906228 37 9

Front cover photograph by Chris McNulty.
Book design by Peter Mortimer.

IRON Press books are represented by:
Password Books Ltd
23 New Mount Street
Manchester
M4 4DE
Tel: 061–953 4009

supported by
NORTHERN
ARTS

BARRAS, LEONARD

Leonard Barras was born in Wallsend. Ever a restless spirit, at the age of 42 he moved three miles to North Shields. It made no difference to his writing, which remained indecipherable. He wrote *"Through My Hat"* from January 1949 to October 1956 as a weekly column for the Newcastle based newspaper The Sunday Sun. It was the nonsense of his nonage. It was his apprenticeship. The disciplines learned then made him the failure he is today.

Over the years, he has written several plays for the stage and several more for radio. He has written a few dozen short stories. He wrote a novel which won a Northern Arts award before publication and was in consequence never published. He has written comic journalism. He has wrestled with television and lost. A BBC2 series called *"Mother Nature's Bloomers"* was hailed as ahead of its time by at least a fortnight. In all of his works, his characters are ineffectual, maladjusted, repressed, unsociable and unloved. They are all himself.

He had a second career in shipbuilding, having been for many years the most inefficient member of the Swan Hunter costing department. But they were kind to him. Everybody has been kind to him. Suckers always get an even break.

That is his message to aspiring young authors. If you can acquire manic depression, schizophrenia and blighting ineptitude, he tells them, you might well have the makings of a comic genius. Unlike him.

AN INTERVIEW WITH LEONARD BARRAS' PUBLISHER

Just how long have you known Leonard Barras?

Well sir, quite a time now. I knew him when his hat brim was still straight.

What else can you say about him?

He makes me laugh sir, and this is not the case with President Bush.

Is this the reason you wanted to publish this book?

You see sir, IRON has already published three of his books. These have been a great deal of fun and lost us a great amount of money, so there seemed no point stopping now.

Any other reason?

*Well now you mention it sir, I realised just how unlike any modern regional newspaper columnist Leonard Barras was. I tried to imagine the current **Sunday Sun** publishing the **Through My Hat** pieces and – well sir, shall I say the thought defeated me?*

I believe you yourself were once a columnist on Newcastle newspapers?

*Just as you intone sir, long spells with both the **Evening Chronicle** and **The Journal**, and sacked from each.*

It is then a hazardous calling?

Hazardous is the word itself sir. A daunting one too. Being called upon to produce lengthy comedy every week is no laughing matter. A man loses his hair rapidly. Such characters as the Omniscient Thurlow Oxxe, Elspeth Ulp, Ambrose Gurtcher, or P. Oscar Struggling make their own demands on a fevered imagination.

Forty years on, what moral message does Barras' writing have for us?

Very little, sir.

Does it have other advantages as well?

Were it not for two of his previous books, my bed would be on a severe slant sir.

An ideal support?

How well you put it, sir.

I believe Leonard Barras' work has been compared to the newspaper columns of Flann O'Brien, who wrote under the pen-name Myles na Gopaleen?

It has sir, just as a bowl of warm soup is compared to a feather duster.

Can you elaborate on that?

Not in so many words, sir.

These columns were first published almost half a century ago, will they now appear severely dated?

Severely dented sir? Not at all.

I said severely dated.

I understand sir. There is a timeless quality to Mr Egbald Knutt's movement to reinstate self-government for Northumbria, just as there is to the concerns of Alicia from Workington, and her husband's ability to put his toes in his mouth, also the writer's involvement in a possible tunnel from Longbenton to Backworth. These are Tyneside settlements incidentally, sir.

Should a columnist not be the conscience of his or her age, the mouth-piece of an opinion unable clearly to express itself without assistance?

You have a way with words sir. And I'd refer you to section two of the book where Barras deals with Professor Beetroot's study on the man who gets his ears wet every time he eats custard; also the author's examination of the back-to-front trousers experiment.

Have there been any academic studies of Barras' work?

He boasts not, sir.

Is there any danger of the man becoming a bit of a cult?

Perhaps you could spell that sir?

C – U – L – T

I would say none at all sir. North Shields has proved itself capable of remaining utterly cultless over the centuries.

Why is Barras not writing a newspaper column at present?

He has nothing to say on the price of fish fingers sir, and there's the living truth of it.

But you expect the book to sell well?

The advance sales are into two figures already sir, and I am not a man to brag.

Thank you.

Again sir, delicately put.

Cullercoats, Tyneside
March 1991

IRON Press has also published the following
Leonard Barras books:

Hailstones on my Father
(comic poems, illustrated by Carole Senior)

Bluebottles on My Marmalade
(prose illustrated by Geoff Laws)

Up the Tyne in a Flummox
(Barras' 1986 Radio 4 pieces,
again illustrated by Geoff Laws)
A joint IRON/Futura Publication

Send for IRON Press' intriguing book list.
Our address is on page two.

Omniscient Thurlow Oxxe writes: So far as disarmament is compatible with abandonment of weapons production, it seems largely to be dependent on the extent to which there is to be a curtailment of the preparation of warlike equipment.

The emergence of universal and simultaneous disarmament may well be achieved if all nations relinquish weapons concomitantly. We are going through a period of disrearmament, and will presently reach the stage of redisrearmament.

Meanwhile, all sides in the world controversy can demonstrate their peaceful desires by the strategic accumulation of atomic and other even more potent weapons.

No Doubt

Mr. Egbald Knutt, of Sunderland, characterising himself as progenitor of the Northumbrian Nationalist Movement, has said that he visualises a resurgent Northumbria 'which will stretch as of old from the Humber to the Forth and perhaps back again'.

The aim of Mr. Knutt's movement is to reinstate self-government for Northumbria, with the North-East dialect as the national language. He made his announcement dressed in what he described as 'dut and claahammer coat'.

"Is this man a chauvinistic nincompoop?" asks Prebendary Sulphur, the eclectic luminary.

Tall Story

The heartening news that there is in existence a League of Tall Women has given me the courage to carry on at a time when I have been unable to sleep much of an afternoon. I just keep murmuring, "There is a League of Tall Women," and I drop off the sofa.

Apparently nobody has ever given much thought to tall women, especially dress designers. Did you know that they are going about in blouses that keep coming adrift from their skirts, and stockings that stop short at a certain point so that every time they sit down their knees pop out? What are you doing about this?

What I am doing is thinking about short women. Life can be pretty wearing for them too. For all I know (or even more than that), they may be condemned to a lifetime of stockings which they have to turn down at the tops like footballers. And in their case, it may well be their blouses that stop short just above the knee. And how many footballers wear suspenders? And how many more sentences shall I begin with a conjunction?

Besides, it is the men in tall girls' lives who suffer most. What an ordeal it is for a sensitive short man who wants to speak endearments to his tall beloved! Her ear is so far off that he has to bawl them in a voice that turns heads in public places.

I am thinking a great deal about this. In fact, since reading that news I have hardly stopped watching tall women. So far, I haven't seen any knees pop, damn it.

I Didn't

SIR, – You recently reviewed Sigmund Zandsturm's 'Teach Your Horse To Sing', which prompts me to point out that in the musical training of horses Mr. Zandsturm was not the first in the field. That honour belonged to the horse.

In 1947, Dr. Karl Kohl trained his mare Pride of Cullercoats to sing the first three notes of 'Jingle Bells'. Attempts to persuade the animal to proceed to more classical works proved fruitless. She boggled at Britten who to his credit refrained from boggling back. In the present state of the arts, there is little chance that the horse will replace the operatic soprano.

MUSIC HATER, Hartlepool.

Passion Thought

Come into the garden, Tennyson said,
For the black bat Night has up and fled;
If Alf had seen you, Mrs. Angeline Platt,
He'd have done the same as his footling bat.

Midnight In Suspense
Chapter 971

What then had happened to the Cawlummi Diamond? That was the question that had Scotland Yard biffled, because of hitting the wrong vowel.

"Have you nothing to work on?" I asked Sir Forbes Story-Storey.

"Only an empty stomach," he said jaundicedly. "How do you see it?"

"It is obscured by your pullover," I reminded him.

Next day found me (with difficulty, as I was disguised) impersonating a stooped lascar outside the Stuffed Duck tavern in the grim dockland of

Annfield Plain. "If you meet me (disguised)," Sir Forbes had said, "do not expect me to speak." What had he meant? Where were his dentures? How had he lost an 'e' from his name?

The day drew on and night came, a development not unexpected to my trained mind. I took up my stance at the bar. It was a long stance, in need of taking up. The Stuffed Duck had filled with dockers and nine had struck (the rest were working to rule) when I noticed that the stooped lascar at my side, drinking his 17th whisky, was (none other than) Storey-Storey.

"You've found your 'e'!" I hissed, which was hardly easy, as the sentence contained no sibilants. There was no reply. Now I knew what he had meant; he was speechless.

He muttered, "Some gibberish, however," and pointed at the bar counter. There unnoticed, especially by posterity, lay the body of Sir Albatross ddunch. Who had done this? Had he any enemies? How did he get into this story? Were Storey-Storey and I one and the same stooped lascar?

(PREBENDARY SULPHUR: "Is this to be continued?" BARRAS: "Not on any account, I have been told.")

Mrs. Chump

My trousers keep slipping over my boots and tripping me up. What should I do? – Lionel, Blyth.

There is a small device, Lionel, on your braces for hitching your trousers up. Alternatively, keep your hands in your trousers pockets. This, however, would preclude ambidextrous activities such as raising your hat and blowing your nose simultaneously.

An Explanation

It was my old M.I.5. chief, Sir Hugo Ivebeen, who caused me to be infiltrated into the Press.

"Never remember," he told me, "that art and life are incompatible. It will be your mission to extirpate one or both, root and if possible branch."

He might have said 'Never forget', not 'Never remember', but I never remember, so either way I am covered (in mortification, by Indolent Assurance Ltd.) and no harm is done, except to the English language.

Next week: How I mixed a metaphor and blew up the leader writer.

2

Today I want to talk about the ancient art of getting all those different colours into aniseed balls.

Has it ever occurred to you just how difficult it is to ensure the emergence of a different hue with every lick? My friends, Marshall Ney remarked (translating at sight), "Person does not demean, as far as one says life is intolerable."

He might not have said exactly that, but what is the gravamen of his words? And which one was this 'one" of whom he spoke? Ah, my friends, the will weakens. Go on to the next bit, for pity's sake.

Daunted, No

The failure of his mission to find the mislaid explorer Colonel Andover Fiste when the lamps went out all over South America, in shameless plagiarism of Earl Grey, the legendary tea-planter, has not abashed the old warrior Major Kalamity.

He is now in the thick of preparations for an expedition to the island of Pattisbobo, whence strange tales have been emanating of a practically unknown race of people who walk about on their heads.

Few facts have drifted through about this phenomenon, but what the major aims to establish is whether these people bounce on their heads, using them like rubber balls, or merely rest on them from time to time as a relief from the more orthodox locomotion of hand-walking.

He is also interested to know whether the blood rushes to their feet when they are down-ended.

Mrs. Chump

We have been going together for 13 years and I have never met her family. I am worried. – MICHAEL, Sunniside.

You have every right. This luck cannot last forever.

Unfair

Tepid on the heels of the news that there is a League of Tall Women comes the report that there is an Association of Women with Big Feet.

We can now await with something approximating confidence the formation of a Society of Women with Ungainly Buttocks, a Union of Women with Protruding Elbows and a Conclave of Women with Bulging Necks.

Do you believe in clubs for women? Only if kindness fails.

Yes, yes. I know.

Come Home

One of the marvels of everyday life (and for me it's a marvel just to get through life every day) is the recurrent theme of the mysterious disappearance.

Each morning sees the case of some such person as Sir Ranelagh Frite, who rises as usual from under the table, takes his hat from the coal scuttle where he left it on retiring, tersely tells Lady Frite that he will be in for tea at 11.30 p.m. as usual, and walks circumspectly out of the front door, never to be seen again (except possibly by somebody who's not saying).

Every year in Britain 243 people unaccountably do not turn up for work, a circumstance which is only slightly less incomprehensible than that of the 12 million who do.

I am not here, however, to offer theories about these allegedly remarkable disappearances. (This week's quiz: What is Barras here for?). What I offer is the thesis that they aren't all that remarkable.

Consider me. I am quite liable to walk down some street, take the wrong turning and somehow fetch up among strange and forbidding people, with the conviction that I have walked out of everybody's life. In any case, all people are strange and forbidding, haven't you noticed?

As a timid little lad, given to sobbing slightly whenever I fell off the school roof, I had a perpetual dread that even as I was in class learning geography I might forget the way home, or more probably that somebody would lift the whole street bodily into the next county.

Now that I have grown older (no doubt about my accuracy in doing that), I have developed rather more panache and most days can arrive home and hit the right house within two or three doors.

Bus conductors are a big help, of course. They all know at which stop to put me off. All I need now is somebody to know at which stop to put me on. That's probably where the Lady Frites of this world have gone wrong. They should see the Sir Ranelaghs to the bus stop. When the bus comes hurtling along, it's up to them what happens next.

After Plumpfellow

Lives of fat men all remind us
We can slumber after strife,
And departing leave behind us
Hollows in the beds of life.

Whither Gutenberg?

Charlemagne Beaufront, the Corbridge fantastick, is seeking to patent a mincing machine, a bath and printing. He believes that these devices are sufficiently useful to deserve re-inventing, except printing.

Settling It

Professor Beetroot, asked to apply himself to the problem of the fool who gets his ears wet every time he eats custard, yesterday in Leadgate University experimented with six monkeys.

Two of the monkeys got their ears wet, one its nose and eyes, and the remainder their ears, noses, eyes, elbows and chins. This is thought to be ungermane to the difficulties of Mr. P. Oscar Struggling, the fool in question.

Professor Beetroot has issued the following report: "A fool who gets his ears wet when eating custard is suffering from self-induced custard-aversion. He may have been frightened by custard in the womb, or more probably his unconscious is disturbed by the unpleasant non-recollection of a thwarted love affair with a woman with some such name as Tryfle or Jelley."

A Harriet Jelley and Phyllis Tryfle are reported to be taking advice from respectively Mr. Gilliefeather Hoote and Mr. Bunfroth Mennadgery, Q.C.s.

Great Thoughts

JOHNSON: Women are like buses.
GOLDSMITH: You mean because there's always another one coming along?
JOHNSON: No, I don't. I just mean women are like buses.

Today marks (delibly) the 263rd anniversary of the birth of dear old Tom Clotheshorse.

In his tiny cottage, Tom used to sit of a washing day, watching his wife as she stood in front of the fire with blankets and shirts and steaming socks hanging from her arms and ears, all because the clothes-horse had not been invented.

One day, the thought struck him: "Heavens above! Am I married to that?"

Thus it came that he might have invented the clothes-horse, which was of course invented 319 years later by Frank Hawsradish of Consett.

So let no damned fool say there is romance in history. Ah, my friends!

Mixed Dates

"I was her 42nd date; she was my 34th." – Letter in 'Woman's Bi-Fortnightly'.

"It has been a wonderful evening, Agatha. If I may say so, the warmth of your presence..."

"Thank you very much, Cedric, but my name's Freda."

"I'm terribly sorry. I thought tonight was Friday. By the way, I'm Henry."

"Of course you are; it's the moustache. You see, Philip..."

"Henry."

"Oh, dear! Forgive me. I'm afraid I'm a..."

"You're a sweet unsophisticated girl, Mary."

"Freda."

"I beg your pardon. I hope this is but the first of at least three enchanted evenings, and that some day I shall call you my own Sylvia."

"Freda. I know how you feel. For me, there's poetry in the very name of Sam."

"It's Henry. Look here, I think we'd better just stick to numbers."

"Perhaps you're right. Goodnight, my very own Number 42."

"Goodnight, my dearest Number 34."

Mrs. Chump

My husband can put his toe in his mouth. Ought I to encourage him? – ALICIA, Workington.

Why not, if it pleases your guests? If the day comes when he cannot take it out, he can fall back on card tricks.

Oh, Really!

SIR, – I have been reading of back-to-front trouser experiments in 'The Tailor and Bricklayer', but surely these merely touch the fringe of dress reform? If you get back-to-front trousers, somebody will have to invent back-to-front bicycle clips.

TOM BLATHER, Low Walker.

Ear Whoosh

A recent conference of gooseneck-benders of 17 $1/2$ countries came to the unanimous conclusion that one of the most grievous maladies of the modern world is Uncontrollable Ears. In 1950, 3,786,366 person-hours went astray when ears were caught in swing doors, bicycle chains and porridge.

What is the answer to this scourge? In a word, WHOOSH. The most intractable ears will respond to the soothing magic of this guggable bilbate. We have a letter from Mr. Osbert Grigfat (somewhere in this heap): "Three days ago, I rubbed WHOOSH on my ears. Now I have nowhere to hang my glasses."

For 'porridge', read 'lawnmowers', if you like.

Sick Transit

I see that a disgruntled old lady has written to an editor (or, as in the case of my editor, an Editor) outlining a set of rules for bus travellers. This interested me not a little, as I am a frequent traveller in buses, when I am not running behind them.

For my part, which is admittedly only a walk-on one, I should like to list some of the travellers, old and young, who have stood next to my seat during my lengthy bus career. I am going to, what's more.

1. The Confidential. This man's range of information about his family's idiosyncrasies, while intended primarily for his companion, is available to anybody within 15 seats.
2. The Fashionable. At the eastern terminus of the 34A (by the ol' Moulmein pagoda), a soignée young woman daily mounts the bus wearing a pencil-skirt of such astounding tightness that the lifting of her front leg on to the step is an operation of untellable hazard.
3. The Informative. Noticing my copy of the 'Stockbreeders' Encyclopaedia', this man engages me in an embarrassing conversation on farmyard genetics and offers to call on me to discuss the sexing of goats. I give him

the address of my aunt and jump off, knocking over a Request Stop. I ought to have explained to him that I had borrowed the 'Stockbreeders' Encyclopaedia' from the library in mistake for the Kama Sutra.

Oh, I have played my part in disgruntling passengers, I own, and sometimes I think I ought to give up travelling in buses altogether. I might still hang around the eastern terminus of the 34A, though.

Terse

Last night, ah yesternight, betwixt her lips and mine,
   There fell thy shadow, Mrs. Prendergast.
That shadow blotted out the kisses and the wine:
   No wonder when the substance was so vast.

Up North

Somewhere in the North-East, believes Mr. Egbald Knutt, proponent of the Northumbrian Nationalist Movement, there lurks a direct descendant of the ancient kings of Northumbria – another Bald or Bert or possibly Wulf.

   Mr. Knutt, although temporarily at the head of the movement, admits that he is not himself a valid Northumbrian. His descent in the male line is through Canute (or Cnut), who completely missed Northumbria while hurrying to meet Harold Harefoot (or Bugs Bunny).

Books

'Coconut Matting in the Modern World', by Farrimond Rowle Topp (Stalemate and Rancid, 12s.6d.).

   A book to be dipped into, albeit deferentially. This is a compulsive volume for all who seek stark verity about the essential coconut mat. Sublime when he is elucidating the fabric of his subject, Mr. Rowle Topp ought perhaps to have resisted the comic urge. Is the coconut mat he wore as a false beard at his niece's wedding consequential?

Shot!

The granting of Test Match status to Pakistan should do much to ease the difficult Eastern situation, reports a spokesman in touch, poor devil, with government sources. Tension might have been eased in Egypt, he adds, if only King Farouk had acquired the disciplines of a short leg.

   The old Imperial vigil must not relax. Only yesterday in Henley incensed oarsmen were on the look-out for an alleged left-wing firebrand who is seeking to stroke ladies' crews.

15

4

There is something I am forever saying and I hope I remember it fairly soon.

Meanwhile, may I tell you how I always seem to be bumping into the kind of man who comes out of a door just as I am going into it? There! – I've told you. What more can I say? And why? Except that another 937 words are required for this week's column?

It's not that this man's sole function is the inopportune arrival in doorways. He also devotes much time to hurling himself off ladders, pulling stiff shutters full tilt into his outstretched nose and backing into people in lifts.

Evolution is a wonderful thing. (Remembered it!) But surely it had some misgivings all those millions of years ago the first time it bade this man stand upright and he, leaping erect, shouted to his mate, "See, woman! No hands and knees!" and fell insensible, having struck his head on the roof of the cave.

Was it worth while going on? That's all I ask. With human life? Or this week's column?

Ridiculous

There is palpably little truth in the rumour that there are plans on foot to build a tunnel between Longbenton and Backworth. So far from being on foot, the plans are in the head of Mr. Phil Thumpable, of whom more or less anon.

"What would be the reason for such a tunnel?" asks Mrs. Blookwith, of whom the same may be said. "Surely the point of a tunnel is to connect two places with a river between them?"

"There is no river between Longbenton and Backworth," is the unequivocal reply of Mr. Thumpable. "How can one build a tunnel under a river which is not there? Who is this foolish woman?"

"Bearing in mind the absence of such a river," Mr. Thumpable was then asked by 'Anxious' of Forest Hall, "how then do you propose to build your tunnel?"

"A hypothetical man cannot countenance a practical absence," Mr. Thumpable asserted. "If Mrs. Blookwith seeks to create a river with Longbenton and Backworth on its banks, that is her affair, and an absurd idea it is."

Mrs. Chump

Alf says he loves me and Tom keeps taking me out, while Ernie showers me with presents. There is also Sam, who is very rich. What should I do? – WORRIED LEILA.

You are doing all right, Leila.

Keep It Up

The only item which emerges firmly as one of the men's fashions for the new Elizabethan Age is the curly bowler. Surely this is going well back, like women's bustles, which always did?

It has been suggested, or will be before the end of this sentence, that the new dress should, as with the earlier Elizabethans, match the spirit of the era, but I don't see why we should all dress as miserably as that.

I am entirely in favour of flamboyancy in dress, which is why I applaud the bowler hat, easily the most daring innovation of the Industrial Revolution, except for Stephenson's inauguration of British Railways with his aphorism about travelling. ("Fifteen men on the dead man's chest.")

There may be more useful hats than the bowler, but none can surpass it for ethereal beauty. I wish Rubens had painted some of his women in bowlers, but they would have had to be pretty small women, which wasn't his style.

Trousers in their modern form were unknown before the 18th Century, when they were invented by the famous botanist Trouser, to prevent the kind of contretemps he records in his Journal: "To the Moors today with Stone*, and collected many Specimens of Moss in Reticule, but Legs much scratched by wild Heather." Heather was, of course, Mrs. Trouser, but it is not known what made her wild, unless she had to carry the reticule.

There are some sociologists who ascribe the decadence of modern society to the cult of trousers, pointing out that in the first Elizabethan Age men had to wear doublet and hose, which virtually obliged them to rush about the world singeing the King of Spain's beard, just to compensate for their ludicrous apparel.

A doublet, of course, is very much like a singlet, only twice as long, and if this discourse serves no other purpose it least it has enabled me to work that in.

This was Roland Stone, who gathered singularly little moss.

Who Did?

SIR, – You recently wrote of the quasi-official practice of lifting the hats of strangers in buses in order to peer at their heads. I protest at your giving publicity to this activity which, if it gains a hold, may well endanger civilisation.

We shall presently have bus conductors empowered to examine passengers' waistcoats for alleged soup-stains, and hordes of officials at rail termini will be raising the caps of bald football supporters and stamping their heads 'Passed Correct'. How would you like to have your sock suspenders covertly examined by a purported fellow-passenger going about on his hands and knees in a tram-car? This is rampant socialism.

LESTER BOUNDAWAY, Jesmond.

Any Time Now

Preparations are going ahead for Major Kalamity's expedition to the island of Pattisbobo, where the strange race of people who walk on their heads are said to live. The major's second-in-command will be young Harry Driftwood, hot from the university, where he took a double first and went on to reach game in 13 darts.

Latest intelligence available to the major is that the natives do not bounce on their heads rubber-ball fashion, but have phenomenally long and rigid ears which they employ as stilts. It seems that the only heads to touch the ground are those which are exceptionally large. This is held to be an advantage, for when a man is pursued by his enemies he can use his head to rub out his earprints.

Teaser 78,865

Which of the following potentates is out of place (and wouldn't you be?):

The Wazir Justnow; the Pounda Suet; the Kachinit Sumwair; the Moldi Cheez; the Wimwam of Karpit Sweepa.

5

The *Wallsend Weekly Buffoon* reports:
Mr. Geo. Bulp, of Lanchester, has built a model of Consett Swimming Baths out of old horse hair. He is calling it Dawn of Geography.

At Jarrow yesterday, Mrs. Freda Oldsock got her elbow caught in Mr. K.X. Krinkle's hernia support. It was her cousin Mr. Frank Rotte's birthday, nearly.

Firewomen in Gateshead will not be supplied with nylon hose. This is believed to be a joke, nearly.

Up North

It seems that a Mrs. Ethel Wrick, who aspires to the throne of the reconstituted kingdom of Northumbria, has already been challenged by no fewer than 91 other contenders.

These include: Mr. Bert Egg, claiming descent from Archbishop Egbert; Mr. Perrishin-Hott, of Monkseaton, alleged descendant of the Flame-Bearer (circa 547); another Ethel – Miss Ethel Frith, whose supposed ancestor was Ethelfrith the Destroyer; and 83 women named Ida, each of whom traces her family tree directly back to the famed King Ida.

There are also Sam Spuggy, J.J.T. Backabitt, Alfred Ycchh, General Damgud-Fellah and Mrs. Potts. This lot thought they were signing a petition to ban ice-cream men's horses from Tynemouth lighthouse.

Verse Again

Awake! – for morning in the bowl of Night
Has flung the stone that puts the stars to flight;
But Mary, in the bathroom, early singing,
Would send those hapless stars more swiftly winging.

Not Tomorrow

Today we bring you the great WHOOSH competition, which it is already too late to enter, because of my bad knee. All you have to do is place the following statements in their order of merit (*sic*):

a.   WHOOSH is the nightshift pease-pudding bender's worst enemy.

b.   No beerstains on the chandelier – thanks to WHOOSH.
c.   WHOOSH three times a day is a damned sight too much WHOOSH.

Send your entries to me, c/o Mrs. Bombable, 837 Denizen Dwellings, Lower Loathsome, together with a pair of newish boots (8¹/₂, broad fitting).

Prizes include 46 inverted shimshocks, 13 graggigles and a two-way pleated oogah.

This stuff may be better next week, depending on my bad knee.

The Real I

"If it had not been for therapy for depression following influenza," a prominent, not to say egregious, author has just said, "I should never have taken up writing." This is another demonstration of how sinisterly powerful modern medicine can be if we don't control it by putting stronger corks in the bottles.

I too am sometimes asked how I started writing. It may be *why* I started writing; I don't catch everything people say. The answer is that one day I was out walking with mumps and pains in the back. It was a day on which the editor of 'Jane Cow', the sister paper to 'John Bull', found himself with a space eight inches by six to fill and the financial news couldn't be got in unless the pound was devalued.

It so happened that I was leaning on his window-sill when he opened it and I fell in, shaking with mumps. They stood me upright to restore the oxygen to my feet and out of my pockets fell 36 pages of notes for a paper on Deforestation in Watford which I was to deliver to the East Howdon Girls' Glee club for a bottle of liniment.

They then found that by printing only every ninth line and turning up the edges they could just fit my lecture in. That, readers, proved the therapy for my mumps and back and set me on the road to the egregiousness which you see today.

So there you have the short answer to how I began. There are also several long answers, but they won't go into a space eight inches by six. There are those who suggest I should be fitted into a space of a different size, but I want them to know that I am still fairly healthy – apart, of course, from bad knee, mumps and pains in the back. And toothache.

Not That

SIR, – If bald-headed football supporters are to be rubber-stamped at rail termini, what is to happen when their heads have been franked all over? Rubber-stamp ink is well-nigh indelible and there must be a limit to the baldness of even the baldest soccer supporter.

I suppose left-wing cranks will suggest that their heads should be de-franked under the National Health Service. We should never have let Marx into this island in the first place.

ARNOLD STOWTART, Blyth.

What Now?

Ever an innovator, Professor Beetroot of Leadgate University has decided to reverse current scientific trends by attempting a method of artificial rain-stopping.

Statistics have shown that summers are no worse today than 93 years ago, but 93 years, the professor feels, is a brief time in the history of the universe, the truistic old buzzard. His aim is to go up in a balloon whenever rain is imminent and fan the clouds with huge mechanical driers.

Later, whole teams of balloons will ascend, manned by specially trained rain-moppers. The prototype balloon is being fitted out and the professor hopes to climb high above Ashington next week. Meanwhile, he is asking Canon Brimstone to pray for rain.

Gee

"Two thoroughbred horses went to a cinema where there was a showing of the Grand National newsreel." – *The Galapagos Sentinel.*

"If rich women can come and glower at horses on the race-course," commented one of the aforementioned ice-cream men, "horses are entitled to stare back in the cinema."

"Democracy is indissoluble," added his horse. "How would the average woman racehorse owner like to be slapped on the flank?"

"She likes nothing better," stated a disgusting trainer.

Axioms

Among possible responses to the boy who hit his father on the head with a chopper and said, "What do you think of modern youth now?" are:

1. "A shade left, son."
2. "Takes me back to the first time I hit my own dad."
3. "Oo!"

Omniscient Thurlow Oxxe writes: How to discriminate against dollar deprivation and yet maintain the essentially stringent level of consumption is the current economic *sine qua non*. I do not advocate inflationary nostrums, but little alternative is signalled in the ongoing fundamental sterling triangular balance dilemma.

And where are manufacturers going to acquire zymbolium, alutex and noxogene? Not from me. I'm clean out of them.

Mrs. Chump

The recurrent problem of the girl with enormous feet is indeed a heart-rending one, but to 'Miserable Millicent', of West Allotment, who writes to me this week, I would say that even the fact that her feet are so big that she can't get them into the office lift will not prevent her from eventually getting a husband or something like one. And my next sentence will be shorter.

Many a big-footed girl, Millicent, finds happiness with a tiny suitor. Little men often have to kneel on the garden wall to reach the beloved's lips for the goodnight kiss. How much happier an arrangement it would be if they could perch (albeit a-tiptoe) on the huge feet of their girl friends!

Of course, the girl with big feet is never likely to meet her future husband on a bus, because she is quite unable to lever her feet into the restricted space under the seats, and if she sits on the long sideways seat at the rear her feet will stretch right across the aisle, causing havoc approaching breakdown proportions to public transport.

Millicent's best hope lies in the open rolling Northumbrian countryside, where she might well meet a stunted shepherd, if she can hire a hearse to take her there.

Any Minute

Only a suitable tide is now awaited for the departure of the Kalamity expedition from Spennymoor Harbour.

Yesterday, the major and young Harry Driftwood supervised the taking on board of stores. These included a patent jimjamometer for measuring the earprints of the natives of Pattisbobo, a stench, a Bolsover gedge-thacket (without which this column would not be complete), five sets of boof-boofs (or boof-booves to the pedantic) and 39 hangers for the scarves of young Harry Driftwood, hot from the university.

Yes, A Dagger

Controversy has broken out again on the subject of the third murderer in 'Macbeth', and we may see the settlement of a problem which has been annoying bardolaters for 350 years. That should annoy them even more.

I want to turn, however, to a more modern work and see if I can interest scholars in getting baffled by it. I refer to 'The Too Too Solid Nightshirt', by Frobisher Kyte, and the enigma is: Who is the Burmese lift-attendant who enters in the second act and cries, "Me? I'm fireproof!"

Is he Mirabelle Froth, disguised as Anstruther Hobbs? Or less probably, is he really a Burmese lift-attendant, and is his name Fah Pruf? Ormswack subscribes to this theory when and if he is sober and maintains that Fah Pruf's father was Barmi Jak and his cousin Rin Tin Tin, a plagiarist Burmese film star.

My own belief is that this odd character is an Irish stage-hand named Alphonse Delacroix, who wandered onstage on the opening night, and the words attributed above are the closing remarks of a ribald altercation with a colleague in the wings which somehow got into the text.

Why was he in the guise of a Burmese lift-attendant? All I know is, he wasn't there when I wrote that second act. Yes, my friends, I am Frobisher Kyte, so why the devil people call me J.B. Priestley I have no idea. In another 350 years, somebody might work it out, or even that I was the third murderer in 'Macbeth', but they'll never hang me.

In A Name

Councillor Mrs. Wallop, Mayor of High Loathsome, yesterday addressed a meeting on the denationalisation of foreign nationals, for want of something worse. Opening with the words, "This contentious wheel has come full cycle..." she was interrupted by five men who rose giving the names of Weel, Hazz, Thiss, Kumm and Fooll-Seickel.

"Surely you have forgotten to bring Mr. Kontenshuss," she enquired sarcastically.

"I am Sam Kontenshuss," another man then shouted, "and I would have you know that I came here without prior arrangement."

A clerical gentleman then stepped forward and said, "I can vouch for that, for I am Prior Arrangement – but I must add that this is ridiculous," whereupon three men jumped up in the front row.

"I suppose you lot are the Ridiculous family?" asked Mrs. Wallop.

"Not at all!" shouted the trio. "We are the Farcical Brothers from Bedlington. Can you work us into your next sentence, missus?"

Knock Tern

Many of you have pointed out an error I made recently, and I wish to thank you and invite you to take a running jump. "How did a tern come to be seen at Wark?" you ask, and don't I know that the tern is an aquatic fowl, not unlike a gull or eider duck? (Eider duck or gull, see if I care).

I should like to bring the famous ornithologist Dr. Guhss to my defence, but he is hanging upside down in the Farne Islands at the moment. What he would say to me if he were here, however, is "How are you, my dear Hobhouse?" He is short-sighted.

He would also say that of course a tern might come inland as far as Wark if the weather were bad, or if it were pretty short-sighted itself. This is what old countrymen (from the Old Country, God bless it!) mean when they say the weather is taking a tern for the worse. I've just done the same myself? Yes.

Still, this is neither here nor there (it certainly isn't here), and I must make it clear that if I have spoken out of tern, it was not my intention to gull anybody. I am now taking a running jump.

7

"**A** woman learning to play the bagpipes used a vacuum cleaner to blow the instrument." – *Bath Times* (by arrangement).

An inspiring experience it is, and one rather frightening to the uninitiated, to see the effect produced by the mad skirl of the vacuum cleaner as wielded by Caledonian housewives.

Mind you, my old friend Hamish Mackerel, the Celtic bard, once told me that a piper who couldn't supply his own wind wasn't worthy of the name. Well, I think he did, but he was speaking in Gaelic at the time. Even less advisable, however, is to try to sweep a floor with bagpipes. You get hardly any dust in your sporran, or so I was told by my other old friend Fiona Ullapuddle ('the lay of the last minstrel').

I well forget the mystification of the guests at a Highland castle who, on sitting down to dinner, were handed copies of the 'Tomintoul Daily Blether'.

"Well, I was told," the 'laird' explained, "that it was the thing to 'ave pipers at dinner, cock."

He was one of those lairds who buy their castles after making a million in South-East England prefabricating delactated synthetic cheese.

Mrs. Chump

Every morning when I wake up, my wardrobe and dressing table are out on the landing. I get my father and two brothers to carry them back, but next morning there they are, outside again. – Minnie, East Boldon.

Do you walk in your sleep, Minnie? Is your back sore?

U Sed It

The Burmese Minister of Culture and Sport – surely you noticed? – is happily named U Win. Yes, this belongs to last week, but they cut it out. Waste not, want not, as my homespun old granny used to say, stuffing me with yesterday's leek pudding.

We shall have a Minister of Sport of our own as soon as we can find a man called Mr. Beaton-Awlendsup.

25

Or This

From the Chinese
Last night I sat with Hoo Plah, the learned man.
The little river is narrow but deep,
Is Hoo Plah's philosophy, and it were better
If man were to end it all there.
This seems very sombre reasoning, but then,
Hoo Plah has a wife, Scree Ching, who,
Seen from whatever view, is not unlike
The horse of Drin Kup, the innkeeper.
Not that Hoo Plah himself or for that matter
Drin Kup are what you'd call Much Cop.

More Elba Room

A persistent correspondent who has written twice points out that in recently quoting a remark made by Napoleon before Austerlitz I seemed to be under the impression that Austerlitz was a man whereas, she asserts, it was a battle, like Ciudad Rodrigo.

All I can say is that the Austerlitz I was speaking of *was* a man. (Well, not quite all; there are 741 more words or they won't pay me.) His full name was Wolfgang Ludwig Austerlitz, although he masqueraded for many years, be it said, under the pseudonym 'Prince Metternich'. He survived innumerable attempts by the Austrian peasantry to assassinate him, until finally the phrase 'Hard lines! Metternich next time!' became a byword among the 'volks' or people in the 'strasser' or streets of old 'Wien' or Budapest.

He was a very ugly man and it was on being confronted by Austerlitz that Pitt the Shorter died suddenly, pointing into Wolfgang Ludwig's face and crying, "Roll up that map; it will not be wanted these ten years!" As a matter of fact, it was wanted by the Emperor of Austria's gardener, who named a potato after it.

As for saying that Ciudad Rodrigo was a battle, everybody knows that it's that little bit of land right at the bottom of South America. Either Ciudad Rodrigo or Nova Scotia.

Ethel the First

Small purple-nosed Mrs. Ethel Wrick of Seghill is pressing her claim to the throne of Northumbria on the grounds that she is the sole descendant of Ethelric, one of the six sons of the great King Ida. In support, she has produced an ancient manuscript purporting to be an historic ballad by Seesic, famed Bernician minstrel. This begins: "Yda, swete lyken apel cyder..."

Asked how she comes to be a descendant of Ethelric if Wrick is her

26

married name, Mrs. Wrick replied: "I am not just a Wrick on my husband's side. He and I are both Wricks. But he yields to the distaff and will be happy to be First Gentleman of my Bedchamber, as I wouldn't like a total stranger in there."

Nor Have I

SIR, – I suspect I know the reason for the reported Customs proposal to subject false beards to Purchase Tax. A man recently smuggled into this country in a false beard worn backwards a genus of rare ant worshipped by unknown Brazilian Indians. Asked if he had anything to declare, he responded, "Nothing except my genus," adding, "My sacred ant."

"If we cut off that beard," the Customs officer said, "you may well laugh on the other side of the back of your head."

The man bowed from the small of his stomach and raised his kneecap, or so I have been told, but I have no idea if I have got it right. It seems unlikely.

GAVIN SYLKE-SHIRTING, Alnmouth.

Yes

Omniscient Thurlow Oxxe writes: What is overlooked by the protagonists of Rent Restriction is that acceptable minima are subject, *ceteris paribus*, to unexempt amenity expenditure, thus entailing substantial corollary rationalisation or even worse.

Realistically, it would seem that no *modus vivendi* is attainable without a *non sequitur*. It has been well said that leaky boots will let the wet in.

Song

> O, Mabel's in the garden singing,
>   Beneath the arbour dew-bedight!
> The greenfly to the rose is clinging,
>   But Mabel's Bach's worse than the blight.

27

8

"Women in the Essex village of Ugley have changed the name of their organisation from the Ugley Women's Institute to the Women's Institute (Ugley Branch)." – *The Weekly Misogynist.*
Events like this, coming vehement on the heels of the rumour that the League of Tall Women is rampant again, glowering down on small Cabinet Ministers, make one wonder whether women are their own worst enemies as well as each other's (as also are men, but misanthropy is held over).

New paragraph. It is the Tall Women who are behind a move to have the entrance to Grey's Monument enlarged. Short women are behind the tall women. The League of Women with Big Feet has won a notable victory in the millinery trade's concession of an extra large size in hats to protect their feet from sunstroke in hot weather. What other kind of weather would it be, you fool?

Another new paragraph. My own favourite headline of recent years was: 'Vicar Likes Felling Women', but that is the end of this paragraph, so I shall hold it over a lighted match, along with the misanthropy.

See?

There are those who are scoffing at Major Kalamity's expedition to Pattisbobo, possibly because he was 451 years behind Bartolomeu Dias in finding pepper in Calicut. What these people forget is that the major has certain triumphs to his name.

Not least among these was his discovery that the source of the River Wattaninny was Lake Plastikmak. For centuries, the Wattaninny had grimly held its secret. Then one day the major, washing his bush shirt on the banks of Lake Plastikmak, upset into the clear waters a packet of WHOOSH (family size).

Three weeks later, the entire River Wattaninny was seen to be filled with filth. There was no doubt whence it had come, for everybody knows that WHOOSH contains the magic ingredient muck!

The major was expelled from Africa with ignominy, but we know, don't we, that they all laughed at Pope Urban VIII when he said the earth was flat?

Teaser 47/Q/6

Agnes is 57 years older than Harriet and half as fat. If Harriet's age is 102 less the difference in their respective ages had she been born in 1857, which she has some appearance of having been, how old is that chap who is asleep in the corner?

Or Jim

Somebody close to me must be interested in 'What Every Girl Should Know About Men', and as far as I know there is nobody as close to me as all that, except myself.

At any rate, a pamphlet with that title fell into my hands the other day, as I lay behind the front door. In it, girls are advised: "Do not kiss Tom, Dick or Harry," and "Even when you go for a ride in a boy's car, you should take a third person; the extra company will add to the enjoyment of all."

It would be an even happier plan, surely, if the girl took along three other persons, and who more likely than Tom, Dick and Harry? They could all count telegraph poles. After all, five people having their enjoyment added to is better than three.

"Mr. Wutherspill, why have you pulled into this quiet lane? What! Kiss you? How dare you!"

"Well, whom else can you kiss, Miss Vargle? Not Tom, Dick or Harry! – see 'What Every Girl Should Know': Page 47."

"Open this door at once! I shall walk home – alone!"

"No, you don't. You can have these three in the back for company."

The swine! But all is well, for the trio turn out to be Bill, Sam and Alfie, honourable men all.

Answer!

SIR, – Why should bald-headed football supporters be singled out for rubber-stamping? Should some thought not be given to adding-machine operators with hairy knees, hammer-toed cost accountants and be-warted piecework counters? These people do a useful job. What have bald-headed football supporters done to ease the export crisis?

We were promised cradle-to-grave welfare. When are new-born babies going to be rubber-stamped? And where?

ALICE GEFUFFLE, Hexham.

J.J.T. For King

Among the claimants to the throne of Northumbria, Mr. J.J.T. Backabitt of Whitley Bay is now foremost in Mr. Egbald Knutt's plans. Mr. Knutt believes that the name Backabitt, or more correctly Ba Ka Bytt, is a Bernician corruption of an ancient English word meaning 'Young Stan has fallen off Bamburgh Castle. Oh, well!'

29

It seems that Mr. Backabitt might be a descendant of the murdered King Ethelred (no, not that one), son-in-law of Offa of Mercia. Historians say that at his first meeting with his prospective father-in-law, Ethelred remarked laughingly, "I decline this Offa of Mercia."

It couldn't have been long after this that he was murdered.

New Books
Some Comments

'Crochet With Ease', by Timothy Flowte. "I searched it from cover to cover and found no mention of how to hit a ball through a hoop." – Admiral Garbidge.

'The Essential Black Bullet', by Elspeth Ulp. "A notable politician lays bare his soul." – Sid Grooch.

'My Life And God Forgive Me', by Ambrose Gurtcher. "Undoubtedly – ho! ho! – black bullets with the lid off." – Aubrey Fritter.

(PREBENDARY SULPHUR: "Has there been some transposition here?" BARRAS: "No." SULPHUR: "Oh.")

Down Under

There is no truth in the rumour that there is to be a tunnel built between Longbenton and Backworth. I have used that sentence before, but it is the same untruth. Mr. Phil Thumphable, the sponsor of the untruth, favours a tunnel rather than a bridge because he feels the building of a bridge would involve the excavation of land.

"So would the building of a tunnel," stated Professor Beetroot, "unless I misunderstand."

"That is your function as an academic," said Mr. Thumpable. "No man can build a bridge unless there is a hole to build it over."

"Such a hole would get filled with bits of paper," claimed Mr. Oliver Bahphitt, the famous park-attendant.

There the untruth rests for the moment.

9

A spectator who volunteered to umpire a cricket match, says my paper, in a hushed voice, smoked throughout, causing great inconvenience to players. This was regrettable, claimed one of the cricketers. I go further, as usual. It was deplorable.

Askance is how we have looked for some time at Australian standards of umpiring, but even out there nobody has attempted to blow smoke in Freddie Brown's face as he was delivering a leg break, or intercepted Denis Compton in the middle of a leg glance to ask him for a light.

When I was an umpire, I once struck a match on the wicket-keeper's stubbly neck and knocked my pipe out on cover point's knee, but I tended to get carried away at women's cricket matches.

Wet Blank

Professor Beetroot's first attempt at scientific rain-stopping last week-end had to be abandoned as the ascent of the balloon was prevented by a downpour.

Better weather prevailed a day or two later, however, when only a tiny cloud was to be seen over the Ashington testing area. Unfortunately, when the moment for the ascent arrived, it was found that the balloon had sprung a leak, and by the time this had been plugged the cloud-mopping apparatus had broken down.

Technicians detected a fault in the Bolsover gedge-thacket and hurried off to Pontop Pike to borrow a nut from the B.B.C. On their return, however, further faults were found in the small-end, the Doddering piston and the glump.

Rain is now continuous over Ashington and Canon Brimstone is wondering if his prayers have overshot the mark.

Never Done

"How can a woman afford to have influenza when a man's only idea of looking after a house is to keep putting more coal on the fire?" – Letter to an Editor.

The scene is an ordinary living room. The wife is crouched before an enormous fire, sniffing. Enter the husband, leaving the door open.

HUSBAND: Shall I put some coal on?

WIFE:	Shut the door. What about getting dinner ready? And what do you suppose we are going to eat? Half a scuttle of nutty slack?
HUSBAND:	Shall I go down to the shops?
WIFE:	That's right – go down when the pub's about to open.
HUSBAND:	Shall I just peel some potatoes?

As there is no answer, he goes out, leaving the door open.

WIFE	(*shouting*): Can you not shut the door?
HUSBAND	(*from the kitchen*): Eh? Ten to twelve, by this clock.
WIFE:	!!! (*She rises and shuts the door*)

Re-enter the husband, wearing an apron but wiping his hands on his trousers. He leaves the door open.

HUSBAND:	Shall I put some coal on the fire?
WIFE:	Shut the door. How do you suppose we're going to eat at twelve-thirty? You haven't even started yet.
HUSBAND:	Shall I open a tin?

Again there is no answer, so he goes out, leaving the door open. The wife rises and slams it. For some time, the husband is heard about the house, breaking plates and falling downstairs. Finally he re-enters, leaving the door open.

HUSBAND:	Shall I put some coal on the fire?
WIFE:	Shut the door. (*plaintively*) It's not myself I'm worried about. I couldn't touch food. But what are *you* going to eat?
HUSBAND:	Shall I make you a cup of tea?
WIFE:	Shall I! Shall I! When I die, 'Shall I' will be found on my heart!

She begins to sob. The husband shifts from foot to foot and wipes his hands some more.

HUSBAND (*finally*): Shall I put some coal on the fire?

There is no reply but a pitiful moan. Exit the husband, knocking over a chair and leaving the door open.

– CURTAIN –

Try A Muff

SIR, – I am a french polisher. I also have the misfortune to be thick-eared. What is all this about rubber-stamping bald heads? I did not serve my time getting onion-stained in order to end up having my thick ears rubber-stamped. We must put up with what we've got. Bureaucracy is too trivial to be left to bureaucrats.

I am not alone with my ears. I have a brother-in-law whose ears get wet every time he eats custard.

P. OSCAR STRUGGLING, Hepple.

(PREBENDARY SULPHUR: "Surely Professor Beetroot has dealt with this problem?" BARRAS: "Yes. Would you like me to repeat the item?" SULPHUR: "Heaven forbid!")

Up North

Stung by the news that Mr. J.J.T. Backabitt of Whitley Bay is a descendant of Ethelred – murdered 796 – Mrs. Ethel Wrick of Seghill has discovered ancient manuscripts by Seesic, the Bernician minstrel, celebrating in song the murder of her ancestor, Bricabrac.

Not to be outdone, Mr. Bert Egg, Mr. Perrishin-Hott, Mr Alfred Ycch and Mrs. Potts have nominated for consideration the murders of their respective ancestors Horsy, Nokneed, Tiddly and Dedrunc.

Even Verse

Look to the rose that blows about us – "Lo,
Laughing," she says, "into the world I blow."
The Rose I know is somewhat less petite;
You'd need a gale to blow her off her feet.

What's In?

Councillor Mrs. Wallop, Mayor of High Loathsome, yesterday experienced her latest disaster in the field of nomenclature when she laid the foundation stone of the new Loathsome Health Centre, Bacterial House.

Seizing her silver trowel, she cried jovially, "Well, I shall give this slab a good thump!"

A man then inevitably rose in the crowd and shouted, "I am Alfonso Slabb and I take amiss that slur."

"Nonsense!" interrupted a woman's voice. "I am Miss Thatslur, and this man is taking me nowhere."

"Certainly not!" said Councillor Seamus O'Bedad. "It is my intention to take you home again, Kathleen."

"My name is Imogen," said the woman Thatslur, "but I am willing to stretch a point."

She and Councillor O'Bedad then took one end each and the point was duly stretched. Alfonso Slabb kissed Mrs. Wallop and declared her open.

"To any suggestion you like," said that large and accommodating lady.

10

Omniscient Thurlow Oxxe writes: With Parliament in recess, forecasts of stability may well percolate retail price media, though not if their particular genre is based on soi-disant 'subsidy' norms.

With market talk of arguable benefits, middle-class consumer tendencies might be partly offset, but not admittedly if wholesale bargaining margins variegate. And what about 'restraint' discrimination, allowing for the inevitable *quid pro quo* demanded by a bear situation?

Going...

Yesterday, with the tide reported as going in and out, the moon on its back and Taurus falling over sideways into Capricorn, all was deemed set for the sailing of Major Kalamity to the island of Pattisbobo.

The major is himself in command of the ketch Imbendin, formerly (a) the Tumtitum, (b) the Agnes Hannah Scuggy and (c) the Invulnerable, under which name she lay ten miles up the Tyne in World War II.

Twenty-nine people and local dignitaries had gathered at Spennymoor Harbour to see the party off. At 7.30 p.m. by young Harry Driftwood's watch (12 noon G.M.T.), the major rang 15 bells and he and young Harry danced the valeta, *vice* the hornpipe.

Verse?

> There is sweet music here that softlier falls
> Than petals from blown roses on the grass.
> The 'music' that is heard when Mary bawls
> Can blow the fuses out and shatter glass.

I Should Know

My remarks on Austerlitz have prompted an ill-meaning man to ask me what I know about the Wars of the Roses, dropping blots on both sides of the paper. This covers an important bit of history, like Napoleon's underpants, which, you may recall, I last wrote about under my maiden name, Lord Macaulay.

What? Get started? All right. Some of the chief battles of the Wars of the Roses were Blore Heath, St. Albans (with interruptions for bad light), Bosworth

34

Field and Mortimer's Cross. It was at Mortimer's Cross that Owen Tudor was routed with great carnage. Riding away afterwards on his riddled horse, the demented Earl of March could utter nothing but "Mortimer's Cross!"

"So's your horse, I should think!" riposted the Earl of Warwick. Later, at Barnet, although there was only small carnage, the Earl of Warwick met his deserts. These things catch you up.

I might make these notes more worthwhile by mentioning something of local interest. Then again I might not. In any case, why should I? Oh, well. Two of the Roses battles were fought at Hedgely Moor and Hexham, Northumberland, respectively.

If you visit these scenes, you will find an old man, claiming to have fought in both battles, who will gladly show you over the field for two shillings a head. For an extra sixpence, he will show you his wound, if you're a lady. What with this and my paper round, I don't do so badly.

Whoosh

WHOOSH (the new heliotrope WHOOSH) is more than a detergent. It's an allergiser!

WHOOSH, slopped in the wash, or knocked back on retiring, or chucked on the garden, or sprinkled from an upstairs window on an unsuspecting head, makes everything allergible.

Treat your woolly vest with WHOOSH and you won't be able to bear it near you. Take seven teaspoonfuls in your bedtime cocoa and see how the wallpaper next your bed has shrivelled up during the night under your stertorous breathing.

And remember! – only heliotrope WHOOSH (it contains muck) makes your whole world filthy.

Into Pocket

There arrived recently in this office a letter signed, entirely plausibly, by a Mrs. Emmeline Pankhurst, of West Allotment, in which she claimed to have invented a billiards cue with a shaving brush for a tip. The advantage of this, says Mrs. Pankhurst, is that it saves the more sensitive billiard balls from being knocked about, and furthermore can be used for shaving by men with very long arms.

I fear that this is what is called an impracticable project. I am calling it that, anyway. I have played billiards in many saloons and actually hit the ball in a few, and in all of them exception would have been taken to the slopping of shaving cream on the table.

Moreover, a man manipulating such an unwieldy shaving implement in a bathroom would constantly be poking out the windows no matter how long his arms. You might as well try to invent a clock with a silent alarm for people who didn't want to get up, or a flannel doorknob for failing to open doors.

What about a safety razor with a billiards tip on the end? This would be a boon to youths with tender skins, or rugged men who didn't want to discourage their whiskers anyway. And it might find its way into billiards saloons for very short men using a very long rest.

On the whole, I think Mrs. Pankhurst should steer clear of manly provinces.

Knee Caps It

Miss Gwendoline Goggling, irascibly disputed Miss Vital Statistic of the North-East, has now threatened legal action against Miss Adelina Nottarf, who is reputedly behind the suggestion that Miss Goggling's left knee is three-quarters of an inch smaller than her right.

Miss Nottarf is herself considering action against the Jarrow judges who took exception to the alleged voluptuousness of her knees.

Miss Goggling may in turn be the subject of an action by Miss Juliette Foist, Newbiggin (Number Five). Miss Foist claims that Miss Goggling accused her of taking lessons from Mr. P.P. Woopy, a Blaydon physical culture expert, so that she could influence the judges by wriggling her kneecaps in a provocative manner.

Messrs. Gillifeather Hoote and Bunfroth Mennadgery, Q.C.s, are watching the situation with interest.

Hurry!

"Over the horizon came a man's hand no bigger than a cloud. This, thought cleft-chinned Sally Sproole, not daring to look into Hugh's fierce blue eye, nor yet the fierce bloodshot one (for was not Godfrey the one for whom she had decided that Hubert...)"

Order next week's copy now! From your newsagent! (Whom else?)

"Twelve strong men lifted the car from over a frightened little brown dog." – Racing and Stock Exchange Gazette.

As I have said so often, how many little brown dogs would do the same for twelve strong men?

It does not solve the much more vexed (who vexes all these questions) question of the countless seagulls which yearly dash their brains out against our lighthouses. Why cannot a commission sit on this? Or at least on those poor orphan eggs?

Up North

Already poised between the claims to royalty of Mrs. Ethel Wrick of Seghill and Mr. J.J.T. Backabitt of Whitley Bay, Mr. Egbald Knutt, of the Northumbrian Nationalist Movement has been stunned slightly by a fresh bid from General Damgud-Fellah.

The general has produced 'incontrovertible evidence' to show that six of his ancestors, Toothpic, Wettblankit, Ethelbald, Ethelhairy, Ethelfat and Ethelooooo, were murdered in one go by being shoved off the Forever For Me cliffs of old Tynemouth by priors from the monkery.

(PREBENDARY SULPHUR: "One moment. Is this a...?" BARRAS: "Yes, yes, a transposition." SULPHUR: Aha!")

Not Banned

'Frank Batterwick – Zumzumosopher Extraordinary', by Jack Pudding (Frowsty and Frette, 21s).

If this book had to be written, which heaven forfend, who better to write it than Mr. Pudding, regarded by some as the leading neo-zumzumosopher. A book that can safely be left lying about for one's children, and one's children's children, and one's children's children's children to walk past.

Gang Awa' Fare

Who was it who said that 'poetry is the consolation of modern men'? Or 'not deep the poet sees but wide'? Or 'My right knee hurts'? (That was me.) Today this column introduces you to the works of the absolutely unknown Scots bard, Hamish Mackerel.

Born on the lonely island of Mphm, reared on the solitary island of Skynny, and messing about on the unfrequented island of Ugh, Hamish Mackerel came from dour Scots stock, and can you blame him? His father was a taciturn man of Mphm and his mother a sombre Skynny woman. His Uncle Arthur, from Ugh, was unspeakable.

Here are just a few lines from Mackerel's moving poem, 'Sair Nae Greet Ma Hashish':

> Saft i' the puir glen, wha gaes ye wi' ma ain?
> Sair noo gaun I maun the hoose abune for nane.
> Sall I greet wi' ma hurtit hairt noo bauchlin',
> Or sall I gang awa' wi' nae sic trauchlin'?
> Och! Fu' the nicht ma Jamie's farrer wroght –
> Nae wae can spiel, I mindit I hae thoght!

It's Blind

"He takes me out five times a week. Do you think he likes me?" – *Letter read in an optician's waiting room, with difficulty.*

"Osbert, you keep fixing me with a look of strained intensity. What can it mean?"

"I was merely thinking, Hildegarde, that the peculiarly ugly way in which your nose turns up could hardly be more repugnant."

"Your observations are certainly arresting. Only last night you commented on the strangely lack-lustre quality of my eyes."

"Like those of a three-days dead haddock, I think was my precise expression. It was on Friday, was it not, that I mentioned how your hair repelled me?"

"You compared it to dank seaweed. Your remarks of Thursday, however, were confined to the bizarre formation of my chin."

"Exactly. It juts out like an ocean-battered slab of rock from the craggy contours of your face. Have I dwelt, by the way, on the overpowering banality of your conversation?"

"On Wednesday, Osbert. You pointed out that the appalling paucity of my intellect plumbed new depths of cretinism."

"Ah, well. Tomorrow night, Hildegarde?"

"Tomorrow night, Osbert."

Quite

"The driver said his name was John Brown, of Pimlico, and a passenger said she was Mrs. Snitchcock Snazzelby. Both names were false." – *News Item.*

But what about the name 'Pimlico'?

(PREBENDARY SULPHUR: "Is this item to be about Mrs. Wallop?"
BARRAS: "I give you my word, no. And there will be no transpositions.")
As I was saying...
Evidence was given by P.C. Wawtogg, answering to Spot. He said that
the woman Snazzelby, or Hatchoo, had driven Driver Brown to distraction.
"You see!" shouted Mrs. Snazzelby, now giving the name of Uffigaam
Unhung. "An opaque case of transposition, to which I plead relatively
guilty, because I am his cousin, twice removed for using foul language on
the upper deck."
Uproar, better known as noise, ensued. "This is impossible," the magistrate was heard to say, almost certainly because he said it, "especially on a
single-decker."
"Not at all," said the clerk, Ingrock Sootch. "Under a statute of King
John the Lionheart, another obscure case of transposition, dear bought is
the honey that is licked from the thorn. This has nothing to do with the
case, but I have sworn, to my mother, to tell the irrelevant truth."
The driver Brown, now claiming to be Green, all down one side, then
rose to say, "All truth is irrelevant." He added that he would state under an
affidavit, if somebody would hold one over his head, that Mrs. Snazzelby's
real name was not Iggliggle but Bommpp.
At that, the magistrate ordered the court cleared, of all charges. "These
people are ludicrous fictions, uncle," he told the usher, Sam Fhootrhool,
who sawed him in two, proving that justice is divisible.

Last Thoughts

1. News from the Far East of the release of Ghaffar Khan will be hailed on
   Tyneside, in spite of a persistent belief in certain quarters here that
   Ghaffar Khan is what the foreman's tea is carried in.
2. Lord Palmerston once remarked (it was either Lord Palmerston or Mrs.
   Siddons; can *you* remember everything?) that nothing is more universally
   true than that nothing is more universally true than nothing.

And there, my friends, is the massage, if not the message, of history. Do you
suppose Voltaire invented volts by sitting back and digging his garden?
(PREBENDARY SULPHUR: "Didn't you promise no transpositions?"
BARRAS: "Yes. Didn't Tennyson warn you at the start that my honour was
rooted in dishonour?")

Among historic potato sacks, is any more justly famed than that worn over his nose and ears by Lancelot d'Erty when he stood on one foot in Durham in 1450?

A new series by Vasco da Robinson on Famous Old Potato Sacks of the North might well, failing little else, be appearing in this column.

Cheap Digs

There is still no truth – and if there were, would it be printed here? – in the rumour that a tunnel is to be built between Longbenton and Backworth.

A further disadvantage of building the bridge which is not going to be built either, Mr. Phil Thumpable feels, is that if you do not dig a big hole for the bridge to span, your only alternative is to erect high lifts at either end to enable travellers to get on to it.

"This would render the bridge useless for old ladies and brewers' dray horses," he told Vasco da Robinson.

"I'm sorry," was Mr. Robinson's reply, "but I belong in the previous item."

Asked how long his mooted tunnel would be, Mr. Thumpable replied that this depended on the distance between Longbenton and Backworth at any given time.

"Surely Backworth is always the same distance from Longbenton?" Mrs. Blookwith is reported to have objected.

"On second thoughts, what is to stop old ladies using lifts," said Mr. Thumpable, answering his own question because he liked it better, "unless they are driving the brewers' drays?"

A Shrinker

Have you tried the new heliotrope and orange WHOOSH? Everywhere, calorifying gauge assessors are saying to each other: "WHOOSH is a shrinker!"

Scientific laboratory tests – performed by scientists in laboratories (in white overalls) – show that WHOOSH is a shrinker, which is exactly what those calorifying gauge assessors were saying up there. Of 187,895 packets of WHOOSH shoved into front doors, scientific tests (another lot) show that nine million burst open, scattering the heliotrope – and orange – WHOOSH all over the hearthrug.

Tests – scientific ones – show that the hearthrugs promptly shrivelled up, thus proving that WHOOSH is a shrinker, as those calorifying gauge assessors knew all along. Scientific tests do not show what the hearthrugs were doing under the front door.

Should Be Shot

Film clichés are not something I have studied as I have gone through life. Mostly I have been too busy with matters like getting my shoes on the right feet.

There is, however, one cliché that I have noticed. (And when I get far enough back to take in the wide screen, my glasses haven't got the power to make out what's going on up there. But that's another matter, which I shall deal with when I get my second wind. Meanwhile, somebody will have to close these brackets.) It goes like this:-

DAWN: "I never want to see you again. Ever."
JOE: "Listen to me, honey. Dawn! Just listen to me!"
DAWN: "It's no good, Joe. It would never work out."
She rushes to the door, pulls it open and hurtles out.
JOE: "Dawn, come back! Dawn!"
He goes to the door. We are faded out on a view of his back.

Now as I see it, if Joe were in earnest about this, he could stop Dawn. He doesn't. He stands there, with his back wearing a defeated look.

I don't call myself a powerful runner. Even as a boy running around the block in one sandshoe, I used to come in tenth out of thirteen. The other three were girls. (Actually, two of them.) But I feel that if Dawn were dashing out of my life forever I could manage something better than fetching up at the closing door and hovering there aimlessly while her feet pattered down the passage.

Even putting myself in Dawn's place, I see it all as pretty improbable. Presumably she is not to know that old Joe is going to turn out so unenterprising. What she ought to expect is that before she has gone 15 paces up the street, Joe will be breathing agonisedly down the back of her neck.

Come to think of it, though, putting myself in Dawn's place, I'd almost certainly find the door knob coming away in my hand. Standing there foolishly, I'd have to make it up with Joe and in the next scene we'd be on our honeymoon with our shoes on the wrong feet at the end of a very short film.

Lost Cause

There is strange and totally expected news from the ketch Imbendin, 700 yards out of Spennymoor on her mission to find the absolutely unheard-of

41

people who walk about on their heads on the island of Pattisbobo.

The major was at the helm, dreaming of his large wife and three little ones. Young Harry Driftwood was below, chopping up the log. To the bridge came Sam Kursit, the mate. Shifting his quid from his cheek, for he keeps his cash in his hip pocket, he addressed the major.

"A word wi' yer, skipper," he said. "Where is this Pattisbobo?"

After five minutes of dreadful silence, the major put about.

Ah, Youth!

As for me, I shall never forget my first sight of a coral reef. October 14th, 1952! The others spotted it fairly early in August, but I had my back to the rail, thinking of the girl I left behind the sideboard in my lodgings.

I had sailed to the South Seas with my companions (boon, they were, both of them), to study the habits of the coral polyp, which I hoped might be pretty disgusting. Commander Crumble was a bluff old blue job, who had sweltered under many a tropic sun (it was the same one all the time had the fool but known), but bearded Dr. Glook was a King's College man. With that beard, did you expect him to be a King's College woman? Given the standards of this column, yes.

October 14th, 1952! It would have been 1951, but we took the wrong turning on Main Street, Cockermouth, given the standards of this column. At any rate, there it was – my first sight of the Grand Canyon! Crumble flung the helm hard over, narrowly missing Glook, and we lurched hugger-mugger into this week's last item (given the standards of this column).

Passion By

> Enormous Ida took my eye,
>   Beside a bus one starry night:
> I did but see her passing by –
>   The bus was quite obscured from sight.

There is one thing I must repeat about this column, amid the welter of things that can't be repeated: it keeps attracting suggestions. Most of them can't be repeated either. Here, however, is one from a purported Mr. Sam Bamboozle of Carlisle. He asks why I shouldn't publicise his patent-pending method of making horses run backwards.

This, he says, would greatly facilitate the work of starters at big races, for horses which shy at being brought up to the tapes could be steered in backwards and would be off before they knew what was happening. Furthermore, jockeys would be facing the wrong way, and those in front would be able to see how far they were ahead of their rivals, as in the Boat Race.

There is really nothing I can say about this and I think I can say it in about 50 words. The Jockey Club would have to devise many new racing terms. What decision could be given, for instance, in the case of a horse which, running backwards, won by a distance which would previously have been called a short head?

Frankly, Mr. Bamboozle, I think Imogen had a better idea when she asked Pisanio for a horse with wings, or it would have been if he'd had one.

Aha!

It looks as though Mrs. Allthumbs, landlady of Professor Beetroot, may come to the rescue of the rain-mopping experiments. The Bolsover gedge-thacket having irreparably broken down, the cloud-drying apparatus is completely useless. Last night, however, Mrs. Allthumbs offered to lend the professor her electric hair-drier. The professor is wondering why he didn't think of that.

Dr. Maypole Pindunder believes that a hair-drier may be capable of dispersing a very small cloud on a very windy day, provided the string on the balloon in which the professor hopes to ascend permits him to climb high enough.

Dr. Pindunder is a hydrologist on a small scale. He taps knees for water.

Mrs. Chump

There are times when I look around me and think that everybody is ugly and hateful. What is wrong with me? – ELLA, Blakelaw.

You are all right, Ella.

Dim View

The epic of the Pontop Pike pioneers and their struggle to give you television is not one to be dismissed cheaply. Not with the licence fee at fifteen shillings.

I bring you now the story of how the great mast was erected. This mast had to be 9,350 feet long, or high, according to whether you were lying down or standing up. It was at an early conference that the brave decision was taken to settle for 9,300 feet as being an easier figure to remember. This was just as well, as the man who had been sent down into Consett to get 9,350 feet of steel (or aluminium – well, it wasn't candyfloss) came back 50 feet short anyway.

The next problem was to get the mast to the top of the hill. At first, two men tried to carry it up, one at either end, the front one using his right shoulder and the back one his left. This had to be abandoned, as the mast sagged in the middle, and the man who was sent to prop it up was young and inexperienced and pushed the whole thing over sideways.

When it was finally got to the top by 100 veterans rushed especially from Holme Moss, there was the difficult task of getting it stood on end. The heaviest man was sent to put his foot on the bottom while the other 99 went to the top end and tried to push it into the air. This also inevitably failed, because the 99 didn't know their own strength and pushed the mast right over and down again on the other side.

So the engineers were left with one last audacious alternative. The mast had to be broken into four-feet lengths and erected by a team of acrobats standing on each other's shoulders. Simple arithmetic (or simple differential calculus) will show that this required a labour force of 2,325 extremely agile men, so you may well understand why the Government was initially reluctant to pursue the project in our present economic straits.

When you have understood that, will you also give a little thought to that man standing on all the other 2,324 shoulders?

Best Scotch

I hae wroght i' the haggis wi' mony a braw lad,
But nane were the sporrans that were there tae be had!
Abune the Skye glens is yon piper's skirl sent,
But I'm nae sic a fool – I'm in Gillingham, Kent.

HAMISH MACKEREL.

Crown Derby

Mr. Egbald Knutt's hopes of settling amicably the claims to the throne of Northumbria have been dashed by arbitrary action on the part of two of the pretenders. Following last Friday's proclamation by Mrs. Ethel Wrick of herself as Queen Ethel, naming her husband Ossie, a trombone plumber, as consort, Mr. J.J.T. Backabitt has announced his accession as King Backabitt the Second.

Apparently there was a former Backabitt (circa 750), who murdered his six brothers, Grogbotl, Beestli, Umph, Orribl, Wassat and Ganninoot, in order to reach the throne, but having reached it died of a surfeit of siblings.

Hot Couture

"One on occasion, he put steaming food in his wife's new hat." – *The Amateur Oculist.*

Thus proving, according to the Bishop of Pump and Bucket, that there may be some purpose to women's hats after all.

He might also have:

1. Filled it with geraniums and hung it up outside the front door.
2. Strained glue through it.
3. Loaded it with nails and sold it as a child's toy.

It was Leigh Hunt who used to dash into the room wearing his wife's hat when Keats and Shelley and one or two others of the gang were there. It was always good for a laugh. One evening, however, he did it when Wordsworth was present. One of those silences as of the seas among the farthest Hebrides followed.

"I was just wearing my wife's hat," said Hunt lamely.

"Her what?" said Wordsworth.

"Her hat," mumbled Hunt. "I was just wearing it."

"Oh," said the Lakeland sage.

Naturally, it was not about this hat that Wordsworth wrote his famous line, "And all that mighty hat is lying still."

The word was 'heart', anyway.

Was it?

The news that 'women's feet are getting larger' probably means that the League of Women with Big Feet will now give the thing up as a bad job. All the same, I bet they are wondering bitterly why M. Dior, who claims to be able to make certain parts of the female anatomy look as though they aren't there, is apparently powerless when confronted by the big feet problem.

A vast upheaval of modern civilisation impends. Lift shafts will have to be broadened. There may well be an international convention to increase railway gauges. Netball nets will have to be enlarged, if I am right in supposing that women put their feet in them. If it is only tall women who do that, shall we see the revival of the Tall Women's Association? Will the Tall Women play the Women with Big Feet at netball in a jumbo stadium?

The upshot may well be a Coalition of Excessively Tall Huge-Footed Women. That would give M. Dior something to think about.

Whoosh

Fear of WHOOSH may be bringing the prices down in the detergents war, but remember – only WHOOSH "soaks spotty'! Soak your old aunt in WHOOSH and pale ale and she will come out covered in blotches.

Home Bound

Back in Spennymoor Harbour, the ketch Imbendin lies forlornly alongside while Major Kalamity and his party try to decide the whereabouts of the island of Pattisbobo. Professor Beetroot, the thoughtless man's Joad, believes it is off Africa; he is fairly confident it is not *on* Africa. Young Harry Driftwood has gone back to the university to borrow Grimsdyke and Foxcheese's Elementary Geography or Geometry; he is not sure which.

The professor's landlady, Mrs. Allthumbs, leans to the view that Pattisbobo is just outside Wideopen. A cousin of her late husband's uncle's housekeeper lived there, she feels, in a big house called Penury.

Big Licks

When I spoke recently of the art of getting all the different colours into aniseed balls, I little thought my words would evoke a tremendous response.

Yes, I was quite right.

For all that (and some of this), Mr. Ernest Highdiddle of Benton writes to tell me that his great-uncle, on his mother's side, and his second cousin (standing behind his father) were in their day (27th August 1901) practitioners of the art.

The process is so secret that nobody knows it. Even Mr. Highdiddle's great-uncle hadn't much idea. But I am in a position to pass it on to my readers and after that, who knows? Still nobody.

The molten mass of aniseed is first poured into the enormous vats by the enormous vatters and allowed to crystallise (or on Tuesdays coagulate) for up to 37 years. This enables the vatters (they are running vatters, hot and cold) to work off a little joke on the journeymen cooks, who (yes) cook journeymen.

"What are you up to?" the cooks say.

"Up to 37 years," the vatters reply, adding, "Ho, ho."

Anyway, you can see there is a lot of good-natured chaff, and this has to be separated from the wheat or vice versa. The separated vice versa is put to one side (it doesn't matter which), for nothing is wasted in the world of the anise, which may be why it is umbelliferous, but you don't want to know about that (either).

So there you have the secret: it is just a big family concern. Very prosperous it is too, although if it is as prosperous as all that I don't know what causes the family concern. Or how they get all those colours in.

Mrs. Chump

Every time I bend over to poke the fire, I flatten my hat on the mantelpiece. My friend Jim tells me that I should not wear my hat in the house. Is this correct? – MORBID MAC.

Normally, yes. But would you rather have a lump on your head? To hell with etiquette, as Queen Victoria said.

Thank You

SIR, – I can vouch for your unpublished story that certain natives of Sumatra wear only a pair of braces, except that they do not wear only a pair of braces and they are not natives of Sumatra. They are natives of Leftover Island, discovered by Captain Bottlewasher, a friend of Captain Cook, in 1780, in the Indian Ocean, and left there by him, and they also wear bicycle clips.

In 1823, a freighter bound for the Antipodes with a cargo of 500,000 pairs of braces for the Australian up-country (to keep it up) was cast ashore on the island when a gale blew up. The natives, who had previously worn nothing but old dickies left by Bottlewasher's men, now discarded these and for 81 years wore nothing but a pair of braces each.

In 1904, another freighter, bound for Haiti with a million bicycle clips, mistook the Pacific for the Atlantic (not surprisingly, as they were both oceans) and ran – or possibly sailed – aground on the island. Ever since, the natives have worn both braces and clips. For many years, serious attempts were made to fasten the braces to the clips, but the braces kept slipping off the shoulders because the clips were attached to the ears.

Before 1904, there was frequent commotion in the British Parliament, with whom it had naturally nothing to do, about the Leftoverans' being quite immodestly under-dressed in nothing but a pair of braces, but the arrival of the bicycle clips altered all that.

My father heard this story from my grandfather, sitting on his knee, an absurd posture for two grown men.

FRANK BILGE, Hetton-le-Hole.

Shelve This

'The Flea Beneath the Skin', by Joseph Updowne – Holme and Drigh, 15s.

Joseph Updowne spent 37 years as a circus flea-trainer and claims always to have brought his charges up to scratch, the facetious ass. His story of how his thoroughbred flea, Sheba, got on to the tattooed lady and caused the first moving pictures is not to be taken seriously.

15

The news that Tyneside engineering apprentices walk out symbolically for half-a-day on Pancake Tuesday calls to mind, albeit faintly, another ancient custom still honoured in the Porridge Quarry at Pelaw. Here, every Dookie-Apple Night, the hapless chargehand porridge-sifter is pursued by a mob of his men and stitched up in a sack.

This dates back to the 17th Century when Titus Oates, the inventor of porridge, got fairly drunk one Dookie Apple Friday and accidentally wrapped himself up in an empty sack. Ever since, porridge workers have commemorated the occasion by stitching up their chargehand as an Oates substitute.

They call this quaint old practice Sewing their Wild Oates, as he doesn't like it much. That historic episode also gave rise to the expression, applied to a drunken man, 'He's as Titus Oates'.

Middle-Aged

SIR, – The story that Lancelot d'Erty wore a potato sack over his nose and ears when he stood on one foot in Durham in 1450 is appallingly apocryphal. Potato sacks were unknown until Raleigh introduced the potato to Queen Elizabeth in 1589, under the cloak of darkness.

Himshimk thinks that what d'Erty wore was in fact a flimsy mediaeval leather 'gwuvwuv', sometimes called a 'thin gummy' (later contracted). 'Gwuvwuvs' (a misprint for 'horsehair pinnies') were certainly worn by 15th Century barrel-shifters to ward off the Black Death, the forerunner of the Brown Ale.

FRANCIS ASHOO, Gateshead.

Further North

General St. Hubert Fitzpompom Damgud-Fellah last night denounced as bogus pretenders the so-called Queen Ethel of Seghill and King Backabitt the Second of Whitley Bay.

Documents ascribed by Queen Ethel to Seesic, the Bernician minstrel, he described as 'piffling forgeries, written on cigarette packets'. King Backabitt's claimed descent was 'a tissue of howling fibs'. History recorded no such preposterous Northumbrian royalty as Grogbotl and Ganninoot. The general then outlined his own lineage through Skynflynt and Oopla.

Queen Ethel asserts that Seesic wrote on genuine 9th Century cigarette packets.

Bygone From Me

Infrequently, to the point of never, people ask me to tell the story of how my ancestor, Nathan Barras, built Barras Bridge, Newcastle. I blush in confusion and recount the following.

One day, a celebrated builder chanced to meet an eminent architect at the corner of Pudding Chare, where they spent several seconds leaping to left and right to get out of each other's way.

"Let's cut out this Marx Brothers stuff for a start, Grainger," said Dobson (for it was he), shifting the unwieldy tome he was carrying.

"The Marx Brothers aren't born yet, mark you," said Grainger (for it was he, as heavily foreshadowed in the previous brackets). "What's that unwieldy tome?"

"Joe Miller's Gag Book (First Edition), if you must know," said Dobson. "Is it true that you haven't built Barras Bridge yet?"

"How can I build Barras Bridge?" said Grainger. "Is my name Barras?"

At that, an old chap who was passing raised his hat in order to prick up his ears. "I am Nathan Barras," he said. "I am a bespoke tailor on The Side."

"Shame on you for not having a full-time job!" laughed Grainger, who had many a time dropped his drolleries in the Bigg Market taverns.

"Sorry I bespoke," said the old chap Riley. (That should be 'wryly'? Quite possibly.)

"Joe Miller isn't born yet, if it comes to that," said Dobson. "Tell me, my man, do you make bridges?"

"Eighty-seven pairs last week!" said old Nathan proudly. He thought Dobson had said 'breeches'.

Of course, he realised it was rather odd when they took him to the top of Northumberland Street and put a shovel in his hand, but as they had brought the Kibblesworth Colliery Band to give him a civic start there wasn't much he could do but go ahead.

And so it came, my friends, that but for old Nathan Barras, the renowned Barras Bridge would not be there today. Neither would I. That is how I recount it. No wonder I blush.

Scotched

And gars yon young Jamie 'bune coves doon in Rum?
Sic a Rum cove is Jamie himsel', traucle some.
"I mind it's frae Eigg is the lassie I wed –
I mind she's frae Eigg by her Eigg-head," he said.

HAMISH MACKEREL.

Mop Stop

Further disaster has overtaken Professor Beetroot's efforts at scientific rain-stopping. Ground tests carried out on Friday, using Mrs. Allthumbs's hair-drier in place of the automatic cloud-mop, proved useless. The hair-drier could not be made to work in the presence of the professor's whiskers.

"There is some peculiar quality in Professor Beetroot's beard," a technician spelt out to the *Wallsend Weekly Buffoon*, "which disorients the magnetic field, immobilising our instruments."

Colonel Hopnatt Kwaver, ex-M.I.5, believes iron filings have been introduced into the professor's whiskers by a quintuple agent. Rain is falling on Ashington.

True Or False

"To be kicked on the elbow by a crow means that you are unlucky in love."

False. When Tim Yellowish, Canon Brimstone's nephew, made faces at a crow in order to infuriate it, the following were the results:

1. A Mrs. Bulge sent for the cruelty man.
2. His fiancée jilted him, alleging that his nose hooted.

Thus, to say that to be kicked on the elbow by a crow means that you are unlucky in love is false, except (a) to the extent that a Mrs. Bulge intervenes, and unless (b) wearing a straw hat makes your nose hoot.

Young Tim was wearing a straw hat (I forgot to say that), possibly because it was a hooded crow.

Give Over

The critic who has just written to say that he hopes to see a certain actor 'in more exotic pants' perhaps didn't mean it, unless he was trying to brighten his monstrously morose profession. Still, he knows now how the novelist felt whose hero 'sat down to a plate of lover and onions'.

'Nothing is to be dreaded so much as long panting', as George Eliot might well have meant to write.

If anybody is looking for a white pudding, I refer her (or him, for I'm no discriminator against men) to Mr. Gilbert Harding, who said yearningly in a recent television programme, "Where have all the white puddings gone?" He received 408 of them by the next post.

What happens, however, if Mr. Harding's plaintive wants become a bit more esoteric? Supplying him with white puddings is not impracticable, except possibly for the G.P.O., but suppose he says in one of those wistful asides that somehow get heard by millions, "Oh, for 17 miles of British Railways track to call my own!" What will viewers do then?

Rise to the challenge, that's what, we few, we happy few, we band of brothers (and sisters).

The Gap

Mr. Phil Thumpable's projected tunnel between Longbenton and Backworth will at first be available only to bicyclists. Asked whether this did not make nonsense of his claim that the tunnel would benefit old ladies and brewers' dray horses, he pointed out that it was nonsense to start with.

"In any case," he added, "old ladies are perfectly at liberty to ride bicycles through the tunnel."

"What about brewers' horses?" asked the *Wallsend Legendary Buffoon*.

"You are soliciting a predictable answer," Mr. Thumpable replied stiffly, and withdrew.

Mrs. Chump

"My boy friend painted 'I love Molly' on my brother's nose." – ISOBEL, Flubbyngton.

I don't understand this. Who is Molly? Was your brother asleep? How big is his nose? What colour (the paint, I mean)? Where is Flubbyngton? And you are supposed to ask me things, not tell me. I am quite confused now.

Yes, But Where?

The Kalamity party for Pattisbobo is still uneasily quartered in Spennymoor until somebody decides exactly where Pattisbobo is. The major, who has no idea, sent an urgent request for information to the Admiralty two-and-a-half weeks ago. Yesterday he received a signal in triplicate asking him to repeat his signal in triplicate.

Three hours later, he received a second signal informing him that, as requested, the medals he had won on board H.M.S. Dingdong in the Rummycove campaign of 1802 would be brought to him by Leading Wren Angela Lurchabowte.

The major has signalled in triplicate that he has no idea where Rummycove is either. Young Harry Driftwood is scraping binnacles, so he thinks, off the Imbendin's bottom.

Gone To Earth?

Given time, I usually manage to catch up with things, and now that I have stopped heading my letters '1953' it has occurred to me to wonder: What happened to chlorophyll?

It is not so long since this green panacea was promising to make me even more adored by women, editor of this newspaper and 58 around the hips. My only worry was that I couldn't sleep much before supper for thinking what the spy networks might do with the stuff. Still, I might have warded off the C.I.A., I felt, by smearing a bit on the gatepost before retiring.

But this great American contribution to democracy has unaccountably disappeared and now there will never be anything to stop me falling over forwards into my inkwell or getting dishpan knees. I get dishpan because women employ me after washing up to bend down and put the pans in the cupboard.

Of course, I have always had qualms (as a schoolboy I once got within three of the set). The foremost feature of chlorophyll was its anti-smell property, present in all plants, so the scientists told us (so the advertisements told us). But in that case what about stinkwort, wormwood and clinging bindweed? What did chlorophyll ever do for them?

Now it may so happen that none of these things has an offensive smell, but I want to say that with names like those they ought to have. On this I am resting my case. It is pretty tired. And if you still don't know what happened to chlorophyll – I admit you didn't ask – my answer is: Senator McCarthy nabbed it for un-American activities.

I would have settled for being leader-writer. I have this cardboard box full of platitudes.

Shortly

SIR, – Just when are we going to get this series on 'Famous Old Potato Sacks of the North', by Vasco da Robinson?

Mr. Francis Ashoo thinks the Lancelot d'Erty story is apocryphal. In my view, there is nothing more dubious than this whole 'Potato Sacks of the North' business and nobody less authentic than Vasco da Robinson. I do not believe anybody ever stood on one foot in Durham, unless it was yourself. The public has a right to know.

'ABOMINABLE', Blaydon.

Naming Names

Councillor Mrs. Wallop. Mayor of High Loathsome, encountered her latest cognomenical uproar when she began a speech in Monkseaton with the words: "I have no use for a party within a party."

A small man rose and demanded, "Is the speaker saying she has no use for me? I am Alfred Party."

"What about me?" cried a second man. "I am Frank Party."

"To get back to the first part of my remarks..." said Mrs. Wallop.

"Is Frank Party the Party of the first part?" shouted Alfred Party. He was then evicted by the doorman, who said it gave him great pleasure to throw a small Party.

"I merely want to say," said Mrs. Wallop, "that my party is stalwart and united. I have a stout party behind me."

"If you're getting at me," came a female voice from the rear, "you should be the last to talk."

Teaser 6 ¾

A man called Joe sets out confusedly from Gateshead and Jarrow.

If little Nellie Kelly, travelling at three miles per hour in a roundabout manner, passes through South Shields at 10 p.m., and arrives two days later in Hetton-le-Hole with a hole in her frock, a hole in her shoe and a hole in her sock where her toe peeps through, is Joe sitting on Mother Kelly's doorstep?

17

"**O**n the bus was a boy whose head had become stuck in a vase. His mother was rushing him to hospital. Presumably to avoid attracting attention, she had placed her son's school cap on top of the vase." – *Esh Winning Post.*

A large woman with a tiny bearded husband might well adopt this ruse to bilk the bus companies. If any of the beard protruded, she could say that was the back of the little boy's neck and they were visiting the barber's after the hospital.

If it were pointed out that his clothes then seemed to be on back to front, she could start to cry and say she had dressed him in a hurry. If it were further pointed out that in that case his knees bent the wrong way... If you dislike these tergiversations, don't forget that we must be free or die that speak the tongue that Shakespeare spake (rustic Warwickshire).

Anyway:

The shades of night were falling
As, with gigantic load,
A trolley-bus came groaning
Along the grim North Road.
Up spoke the ancient clippie:
"You'll have to move up, please;
And grown-ups take the small ones
And place them on your knees."
A girl of stunning beauty
Then seized a little chap
Who, sighing, snuggled closely,
And nestled in her lap.
"My little man's not scared, then,"
Said she in accents sweet,
"Of Jesmond's murky shadows
Or dreadful Pilgrim Street?"
He answered downright smartly:
"Me? Frightened of the dark?
Not likely! I'm a jockey
Just come from Gosforth Park."

Dry Rot

Called in by Professor Beetroot, Dr. Finicky, statistician at Leadgate University, has pointed out that one of the reasons for the failure of the Beetroot rain-mopping experiments is the lack of substantive connotations. "Figures indicate," Dr. Finicky told the professor, "that when the sum of inherent attributes has not been analysed over a sufficiently assessable period, it follows, *per se*, that their value is relatively negated."

Professor Beetroot does not disagree with this, but feels bound to point out that his name is not Percy. Meanwhile, the rejection of Mrs. Allthumbs's hair-drier as a possible substitute for the broken cloud-mop is causing ugly comment. Why should a hair-drier fail to work in the presence of the professor's whiskers?

Rumours are rife (when are they otherwise?) in Leadgate that the professor has worn a false beard all these years, and that Dr. Finicky is omniscient Thurlow Oxxe incognito.

No Louvre Lost

"Genius and insensibility are mutually exclusive," a critic has just said. I see what he means, at the second attempt. Just how easily a thoughtless remark can set alight these touchy prodigies is well exemplified by the classic row between Balzac and Flaubert.

Spotting Balzac on the Left Bank one day, Flaubert shouted (he had to shout as he was on the Right Bank at the time): "Tenez vos chevaux, mon vieux coq!", meaning "Hold your horses, old cock!" for he wanted to ask if it was true that Sand had invented egg-timers.

Balzac, however, thought he said, "Tenez vos cheveux!" ("Keep your hair on!"), a rather unfortunate mishearing, Balzac being as bald as a billiard ball.

The thing was never patched up, of course, and French literature has been the poorer for it, for Flaubert wanted to use that 'egg-timer' stuff to give 'Madame Bovary' a comic ending. What? It had one anyway? Oh.

No Filverfmiths

SIR, – My great-great-great-great-grandfather was an ostler and I have in my collection of antiques one of his 18th Century ostles, albeit with the handle broken.

I also have a magnificent teak wharfinge, made by a city wharfinger circa 1751, five tallow chandles, a set of favours worked by a master currier, a hand-knitted coop made by Jno. Blenkinfop, cooper, in 1785, and a cheese monged by one of the 18th Century's most famous cheesemongers, Jofeph Famfon of Mofley Street.

OSWALD FOLDUP, Corbridge.

At Last

Mr. Geo. Bellowing of Tynemouth was one of five readers of this column (five? – on to double figures!) who did not understand its antediluvian book review about zumzumosophy. May I explain, starting on the next line?

Zumzumosophy may be said to represent an outlook which had its earliest expression in the belief that suspenders are not necessary to keep up the human sock. Not only may it be said; it just has been.

It was brought to the North-East by old Frank Batterwick, who turned from sock-suspension to trouser engineering late in life and devoted his declining years to the theory that trousers, instead of having turnups on the bottom, should have turndowns on the top, the principle being that turndowns are less likely to turn up than turnups are to turn down.

This is zumzumosophy proper and it was born because by the time he had reached old age, Frank Batterwick had been well-nigh reduced to despair by the kind of woman who taps you on the shoulder and says, "Your turnup is turned down."

Resigned as he was to being told that his tie had slipped, or having fluff picked off his waistcoat, he could not bear with equanimity (or any other way, damn it) the thought of going through his few remaining days constantly hopping about on one leg while adjusting the turnup on his other.

Of course, the Batterwick pioneer trousers with the turndown top were laughed to scorn, or fairly close, on their inception, but we should not cavil, my friends, except in the privacy of the home with drawn blinds. As I have often said, decency is indecency's conspiracy of silence. So, to be fair, did Shaw.

Mrs. Chump

I told my boy friend that a weak handshake is a sign of a weak character. Since then, he has fractured my father's wrist and three of my brother's fingers. What can I do? – JILL, Birtley.

See that in no circumstances does he accede to the throne of this mighty realm.

L ate again, here are Raggle-Taggle Lenny's forecasts for 1956:
Jupiter Subjects. On February 20th., your peculiar habit of standing too close to a door when you pull it open will lead to your dealing yourself a severe blow on your nose, occasioning bloody, albeit less than mortal, injuries.

Mars Subjects. Arriving at the theatre on April 11th., you will find a large confident man in your seat. Persuading yourself that it was your mistake anyway, you will turn and stalk blindly out, leaving your hat and walking into the commissionaire.

Moon Subjects. You will run after the wrong bus all the way up Grainger Street on June 22nd. Sent back, you will join the wrong end of the wrong queue.

Mercury Subjects. On September 10th, a perfectly sound ceiling you are distempering will collapse. During the next few days, two clocks, four hat-stands and a middle-aged female caller will come apart in your hands.

Venus Subjects. During the month of October, you will stand on 83 feet, travel eleven times past your station, go into 37 wrong rooms, insult seven people with perfectly innocent intentions, put your head through a floor and wake up in the middle of every night wishing you could start your accursed life all over again.

Saturn and Uranus Subjects. Here comes December 31st., but don't look forward to next year. For your sort, things never get better.

Of course, all the foregoing prognostications apply to seven different subjects. The most any one person can get is one of them. Except Raggle-Taggle Lenny himself. He'll go through the lot by January 21st and be well on the way to improvising 200 more.

Battle Cry

Major Kalamity, still motionless in Spennymoor, has replied to the Admiralty that he lays no claim to the medals he is reputed to have won off Rummycove in 1802. All he wants is information regarding the whereabouts of the island of Pattisbobo.

In response, there arrived in Spennymoor yesterday a vast package containing detailed maps of the Rummycove sea area, with a small asterisk on one of them indicating that 'Admiral Shimmering-Dulally, on board H.M.S. Dingdong, fell here in 1802'.

A footnote adds that he was picked up by A.B. Stoop and carried to the poop, in order to provide a ready rhyme should a latter-day Poet Laureate want to commemorate the occasion.

Clock Out

SIR, – Like your worthy self, I am an old man now and, being of a philosophical turn, have learned to live with my troubles in a particularly graceless and resentful manner. One of these concerns the hackneyed ballad 'My Grandfather's Clock'. I daresay you know how it goes, although you, of all people, will bear in mind that it won't go at all unless you wind it up.

It is with the third line, "It was taller by half than the old man himself," that my carping begins. The song tells us that "it was bought on the morn of the day that he was born," so at what stage of the old man's life was the clock taller by half than he? And in view of the fact that "it weighed not a penny weight more," are we to assume that the old man was the same weight for 90 years?

But this was a remarkable clock all round. "It struck twenty-four when he entered at the door with a blooming and beautiful bride." We are not told whose bride grandfather was entering with. All the same, he must have been less than human if he didn't lean her up against the sideboard while he had a look at a clock that could strike twenty-four.

"It rang an alarm in the dead of the night." I have had clocks like that myself, but not for long. This alarm, however, was "an alarm that for years had been dumb." What is one to make of this?

In short, this grandfather's clock seems to have been an eccentric and completely unreliable timepiece. I am glad to say, mind you, that better models are being made nowadays.

I enclose my card.

W.X. PULLOVER, Dedrite Clock Co., Gateshead.

Sort Out

Mr. Phil Thumpable has replied to a further claim by Mrs. Blookwith that as there is no river between Longbenton and Backworth the building of a tunnel is pointless. "Tunnels under rivers have little drops of water falling into them all the time," Mr. Thumpable told the permanently unreceptive *Wallsend Weekly Buffoon*. "With my tunnel, this will be impossible."

The question of brewers' horse-drawn drays having been raised again, Mr. Thumpable conceded that in addition to old lady bicyclists, brewers' horse would be allowed through the tunnel, provided they left their drays behind. They could then return by surface route to fetch the beer.

Apologise Nothing

Those scornful correspondents (still running into single figures) who have visited public libraries and doubt my story of the literary quarrel between Balzac and Flaubert seem to think I was referring to Honoré de Balzac and Gustave Flaubert, and so I was if I could have got away with it, but I want to say... I shall say it by beginning a new paragraph.

I want to say that of course the two I had in mind were Geordie Balzac of Ashington and Joe Flaubert (né Ging) of South Shields. Now that I've said it, you may ask (so I hope, having prepared the answer) why they conducted their argument in French. Who was Sand? How did "Madame Bovary" get into it? (All right – *what* was sand?)

The answer is that neither Geordie Balzac nor Joe Flaubert could speak French, so are you surprised they misunderstood each other? Well, then. They didn't speak good English either. In fact, they spoke rotten English.

One further question, then turn to Page Four. Do you understand what all this is about? If not, ask at the Backnumbers Department, my symbolic home. Another thing – this *is* Page Four. I must close now, dear granny, as my pen is leaking. Good bless you all. As this leaves me.

19

"**M.** Reynaud is the best man the French could choose. His English is as good as his French." – *Daily Xenophobe.*

In the impenetrable Carpathian state of Umbrage, the best man for the job is Mr. Thinstiletto, for his Damnatian (the language of the other impenetrable state of Damnatia) is as good as his Umbragio. What they will do when he dies (he is only 137, which is pretty young by Carpathian standards) nobody knows, unless they can find an Umbragian of English descent, whose word will be as good as his bond.

Upper Crust North

Further documentary evidence has emerged in the struggle for the throne of Northumbria. Mr. Hercules ffillett, curator of the Wallsend Busmen's Pea and Pie Museum, has sent to General Damgud-Fellah manuscripts purporting to be the work of the ancient Welsh bard Cadwatter.

These seem to show that the general's ancestor, Bigbonss, was an undoubted King of Northumbria, and the words "Wy doen every boddey clep me bigg edd?" which appear in them, will henceforth be incorporated in the Damgud-Fellah family motto.

The general looks forward to having himself crowned King St. Hubert Fitzpompom the First. The Bishop of Pump and Bucket will officiate.

Don't Ask Me

Lovely old Leadgate is seething with speculation over the Beetroot beard. "If the professor's whiskers are composed of genuine hair," asks Prebendary Sulphur, the pop-up pundit, "why is it that a hair-drier will not work in their presence?"

On the other hand, Mr. Barker-Drowte, Mr. H.L. Glooge and Miss Thomasina Berry-Berry-Berry have pointed out that the hair drier's inefficacy may simply indicate that it is not a genuine hair-drier.

"If we have a non-genuine hair-drier applied to non-genuine hair, we cannot expect adequate statistical data," states Dr. Finicky, Leadgate University's leading (by a long head) statistician.

The professor, waiting in Ashington for rain, yesterday got his beard wet when he was gazing at a local beauty spot and was pushed playfully by the local beauty into a bird bath. He dried it by running on the spot.

61

Toujours

"My husband always kisses me before he goes to work and when he comes home at night, and he always raises his hat to do so." – *Letter to an Editor.*

But what does he do in between?

I am reminded of one of the notes Elizabeth Barrett Browning used to leave on Robert's pillow:

You may sometimes stoop to habits mean and shady,
But unless you're downright rotten to the roots
You will never raise your hand to strike a lady –
Why should you if you're wearing hobnailed boots?

Vile Anyway

The other day I bumped into an old scientist acquaintance, the string having come off my glasses again, and not unnaturally, my friends, we fell a-reminiscing. A kindly passer-by stood us up, however, against a lamp, and presently my friend was telling me just how he would re-arrange the human body if he had a free hand.

"I would start," he said, as I re-arranged my own body, for slumber, "with a loose gullet."

"You've already started with a free hand," I said, laughing behind the lamp. (It was a light laugh.)

But he left me with a thought running through my head, and nothing to make a race of it. How many of us, I mused, have not dreamed of improving on nature, moving it up and down and perhaps crossways a bit? Why, for instance, do you suppose the humble moth has the design of a fearful dragon on his wing? Did you, in fact?

My friends, my friend Professor Wrottin in his 'Animal, Vegetable or Malcolm Muggeridge', says that the moth does this to disconcert his enemies. Of course, you may think the moth could disconcert his enemies (nay, infuriate them) by staying indoors and getting into their winter underwear, but what do you and I know about such environmental phenomena, dragged up as we were in the mean streets of Jesmond with nothing but bread and dripping to lie down on of a cold night?

No, my friends! My friend (the one I met in Paragraph One) was wrong. We can safely leave the human body to Old Mother Nature, plus a bit of iron mixture for the blood, some stomach powder, cough emulsion, hair tonic and elastic knee-pads.

Mrs. Chump
Your Coronation Braces

The thing to do to bring your braces into line with current patriotic trends is to have them dyed red, white and blue. Nothing is more sombre or cramping to a man's social style than the gloomy brown braces so many affect.

You will certainly be the cynosure of all eyes if, when you take off your gloves and bowler at your firm's Coronation Swimming Gala, you are able to stand revealed in old gold swimming trunks supported by braces of noblest red, white and blue.

And at the business conference, the man who is twanging braces of a dingy grey will never get the order. That goes to the chap looking confidently out at the world from behind the bright red, white and blue braces into which his thumbs are so boldly stuck. And have you thought of royal purple sock suspenders?

What Is This?

SIR, – Frank Batterwick's closest associate when he introduced zumzumosophy was certainly not Mildred Gassbrackit, as the ill-informed claim. She it was who became a Kandelstick when she married Willie of that ilk, he being better known for his ximxomulism. Frank Batterwick was 93 at the time. And what about Rudolph Pipp?

HARRY CRASS, Blyth.

It Is

The *Wallsend Weekly Buffoon* reports: Mrs. Crinch of Gosforth called out her cat Einstein when she found the Fire Brigade stuck up a tree... Mr. Tim O'Clavverbogle, aged 93, of Ryton, doesn't remember the Tyne being frozen over. "The silly ****** doesn't remember his own name," said his wife, Francoisine... Three Longhorsley brothers named Smith, Wilkinson and Grey claim that their combined ages are 976. They further claim that this is ridiculous.

"An unknown girl has been chosen as 'Miss Grapefruit' because her face symbolises the fresh clean qualities of that fruit." – *Rutland Bugle (with Triangle Supplement).*

Gratifying though it be that a tall straight English girl, presumably with round yellow face, has been chosen for this exotic role, it should not be forgotten that there is many an English fruit and vegetable of equal glamour to these garish foreign products.

On all sides, there are long thin red girls strikingly symbolic of our island rhubarb. while English plum-type beauties abound in the mottled damsels you meet in office and omnibus, leaving the sliding doors open and getting their coats under your feet on the stairs.

I have even misheard it said that the recent Turnip Queen of Rothbury was chosen for her fascinating resemblance to King Alfred. If that's a potato, shut your face.

Hot Feet

Landbound in Spennymoor, Major Kalamity is desperately seeking some means of convincing the Admiralty that he cannot possibly be Admiral Shimmering-Dulally, with whose medals Leading Wren Angela Lurchabowte is reported to be coming pell-mell from Whitehall.

In a signal on Tuesday, the major asked: "If Admiral Shimmering-Dulally fell at Rummycove in 1802, with cannonballs in his chest, head and kidneys, how can I be he? Is it possible that I am 205 years old and full of holes?"

The Admiralty has replied that it views with some reserve his claim to have reached that age and has asked him to complete in triplicate 17 forms showing why his half-pension should not be stopped. Commander Badstuff is coming pell-mell after Wren Lurchabowte, partly to look into the matter and partly because he is hopelessly in love with her.

Good old J.H.

WHOOSH washes spotty! If you soak your whites in WHOOSH, they will come out spotted. But if you add the wonder ingredient whose name scientists are still working on, they will no longer be spotted. This is because WHOOSH also washes unspotty (or unwhite). The choice is yours!

Mr. J.H. of Hebburn boiled his wife's vest in WHOOSH. Her vest ran up the small of her back and she hit him with the clothes-prop. WHOOSH is a shrinker, which is what makes the small of the back smaller. The small of your back could be eliminated. Scientists are working on it.

Busking Sharks

One thing I feel I shall never make much of a shot at is playing a tune on a bicycle pump. I could make a much better shot at telling you all the things I couldn't make much of a shot at.

Yet there is a man who stands alongside cinema queues in Newcastle singing 'Souvenirs' and accompanying himself on the inflator. I think it is 'Souvenirs', but it may be 'The Road to the Isles'; no busker is permitted by the rules of his craft to play a tune which is recognisable by the lay ear.

At that, of course, a man playing a bicycle pump is off a good mark. If you want to play a tune which nobody is going to recognise, you could hardly pick a better wind instrument than a bicycle pump.

It must have taken Newcastle's other queue musicians, with their more orthodox melodions and tin whistles, years of burdensome practice to acquire the perfection of never quite playing a tune. I have enormous sympathy for these men, short of actual cash. I picture one of them at home, moodily toying with his breakfast, caring not that the noonday sun is shining merrily outside.

"Terence," says his wife, pressing him vainly to a fifth rasher, "what strange *ennui* possesses you?"

"Lydia," he confides, "yesterday in the Paragon queue, somebody recognised 'Springtime in the Rockies'." Rising, he staggers blindly out, knocking over a vase containing 2,000 threepenny bits.

There are no worries of this kind for the man playing the bicycle pump. To him, nothing is impossible. Unless one day somebody asks him to pump up a bicycle.

Mrs. Chump

"My fiancé never calls me anything more endearing than 'old sock'. How can I stop this?" – Cynthia, Sunderland.

Each time he says this, my dear, you should reply laughingly: "Terence (or Jimmy), I'm darned if I'm an old sock!" Incidentally, I've had a letter from a young man called Jimmy whose fiancée Louise calls him Terence. I wish you four people would sort this out.

Where?

SIR, – Mr. Harry Crass demolishes his own argument by dragging in the name of Rudolph Pipp, who did no more than flirt with zumzumosophy.

Mildred Gassbrackit was 27 when she fell under Frank Batterwick's spell. Jack Pudding was well-qualified to write the biography of the arch-zumzumosophist, but it was Willie and Millie Kandelstick who put zum-zumosophy where it is today.

FREDA LAW-LUMMY, Sunderland.

Blue Blood

"Vacant: Homely lodgings for two gents, or police." – Advertisement.

> *If it's thoroughbred blood that you're after,*
> *Then you'll not find a drop in the Force,*
> *Till you come to a mounted policeman –*
> *And it's not in the cop but the horse.*

Teaser Minus 43

Which of the following is pointless:

1. Rodin is a French girls' school.
2. Anchovy is a hermit.
3. Cassocks roam the Steppes.

Tailpiece

Sandy Goosegrass, the Low Fell runner-behind-buses, admits that his first attempts to pursue buses were half-hearted. "They were more or less a joke," he tried to tell the *Wallsend Weekly Buffoon*. "Then I realised that if this machine age was not to destroy us it behoved men like me to run after buses with some earnestness."

His initial bus chases were more or less retaliatory. He pretended to resent the action of a Heworth bus in running behind him, sounding its horn. Because of this, when he first ran behind buses he used to utter a cheerful "Parp, parp!" Since he took to more serious bus-pursuing, however, he reserves his "Parp, parp!" for Bank Holidays.

21

The Recorder said: "I am sorry for you, but to carry a half-brick is against the whole kindly nature of the English people." – *Wholesale Carnage Weekly.*

Such kindliness is, of course, hardly to be expected elsewhere. Once across the Border and the inoffensive Englishman walks in hourly dread of those grim Welshmen and Scots, laden as they are with lethal leeks and pibrochs.

Moreover, only Englishmen can be said to have a true sense of humour or the knack of handling women, which is the same thing now I come to think of it, although that is not what I came for. And did you ever see a Glaswegian pat an alligator? Who was the Frenchman, my friends, who said (translating loosely, as these Gallics do): "I like the English, in spite of their ugly hats"?

This does not prove my point and it is not even the quotation I was after, but of course a goshawk beats not at a bunting, as my granny had it, and she was welcome to it.

Fare Play

A traveller approached a railway station booking office and said, "One to Manchester."

"I'm happily married, sir," replied the lady booking clerk demurely, "and my name is not Chester."

Beard Bath

The Leadgate University authorities have asked Dr. Finicky why it is that although 2.34 inches of rain have fallen, among other things, on Ashington since Professor Beetroot's arrival there, there is no evidence that he has mopped up any of it.

"All that he has mopped up," states Wtlgdbn Pdcljs, a vowel-less citizen, "is the water in Mrs. Wibduck's bird bath."

The bird bath, swollen by recent downpours, was again fallen into twice yesterday by the professor, his whiskers being severely drenched on both occasions.

Dr. Finicky feels that this disposes of the notion that the whiskers are false. "Only a genuine beard could stand up to such a buffeting," he told this column, repeating it until it sank in.

Right Dress

SIR, – You have completely missed the point in your exposition of zumzumosophy. It is true that old Frank Batterwick was set afire by the triumph of turndowns that could not turn up over turnups that could turn down. But even more inspiring was the revelation that turndowns could not harbour old bus tickets.

The glory of zumzumosophy is that it is utilitarian as well as decorative. Frank Batterwick might well be said to be the pioneer of aesthetically functional trousers.

ALF. TUTTUTT, Penrith.

Leave of Ticket

Today I want to speak of a friend of mine who has had a rotten deal from life, quite apart from being a friend of mine, that is. For many years he lived next to a bus stop. Every ten minutes, winter and summer (and damn it, spring and autumn as well), a bus pulled up at his gate and shot off a crowd of passengers, who promptly screwed up their tickets and flicked them over the hedge into his garden.

It would have made no difference if he had not been a keen gardener (except to his garden and this story). But was there anything, he asked me, more disconcerting, when kneeling over your oxymorons than to be covered in tickets six times an hour? They might have been zeugmas; he wasn't a very literary gardener.

But he was a doughty fighter and he devised the fine plan of building his hedge higher. Such is the tenacity of the travelling public, however, that they made it a matter of honour to get their tickets over at any price. Higher and higher my friend elevated his hedge, until he had to engage a firm of contractors to keep it pruned, not unlike the painters on the Tyne Bridge. Still the tickets flew over.

The end came when a man entered his garden one day and said, "I have just thrown a ticket over here. It was a return. May I have it back?" My friend struck him a terrible blow with a freshly-picked synecdoche and rushed off to the estate agent's, selling at a tremendous loss.

And so, readers, if you ever feel tempted to screw up your bus tickets and flick them over a garden wall, please refrain. Drop them down the back of the neck of that lady in front. Or take a healthy walk to the Tyne Bridge to watch the painters pruning it.

Hot News

"The effect of ten M.P.s going through a division lobby is equal to that of a one kilowatt fire." – *Yes, another news item.*

This is why Government correspondence always bears the message OHMS, reports a little-known electrician.

Recorders of this age may well repeat
That during fuel cuts in 'fifty-three,
You warmed your toes by drawing up your seat
And toasting them against your prone M.P.

Up North

It seems that after a lapse variously put at many centuries and six months, Northumbria may again be ravaged by internecine warfare. Under the rival banners of Queen Ethel and King Backabitt, angry adherents are beginning to gather. Both sides are hourly expected to march out of their strongholds at respectively Seghill and Whitley Bay, proclaiming self-government.

One of King Backabitt's spies, returned from a mission to Scotland to see how these things are done there, suggested a variant on the theme of setting fire to letter-boxes. There will therefore be a campaign of puncturing postmen's bicycles.

Queen Ethel's followers, it is said, will respond by removing postmen's left bicycle clips, if they can find a hygienic way of doing it.

In Case

'Through Wallsend With My Ballpoint', by Leonard Barras (Torpid and Fungoid, 1s.3d).

Entirely underdue is a standard work on Wallsend, or even on ballpoints, and certainly on ugly reprehensible old Len. Who could fail to be unmoved by his oxymorons, zeugmas and synecdoches?

No wonder I couldn't make anything of the railway dispute. I thought a 'lodging turn' was a facetious boarder.

Here It Is

FAMOUS OLD POTATO SACKS OF THE NORTH
by Vasco da Robinson

About 200 years ago (200, let us say), there was a little house hard by a ramshackle old official building (hard) by St. Nicholas's Cathedral, Newcastle. That little house is no more, but you can still see the Town Hall. If you had been passing that house one day in 1754, you would have witnessed a scening move if you had been the kind of person who transposes on finding himself in a story like this.

Timothy Yool, a handsome young man with the world at one of his feet, for he was far from ambitious, was bidding farewell to Lady Phoebe Damp, the titled girl (I did say 'Lady'?) whom he loved in spite of herself. Her father, Lord Sopping, would not hear of their marriage, for he was a deaf old coot, and so Timothy was walking slowly away to sea. Let the others run! He was far from ambitious!

(PREBENDARY SULPHUR: "What has this to do with old sacks?" BARRAS: "That should be 'old socks'. Now read on.")

"Will you not give me some token before you go?" cried Lady Phoebe, sobbing into the Cloth Market.

Standing on his left leg, Timothy removed his sock, almost certainly the right one. Pressing it into her hand in the shadow of the Town Hall, he kissed her on the front portico and made off (with a marked limp) down to the Quayside.

Tearfully the girl pinned the sock into her corsage beside the red rose, which was wilting anyway, and returned to her father. "This is the end of the world," she said.

"It's Westgate Road," he replied. "It always seems like that."

For twenty years she wore the token. Clayton and Grainger came and overhauled the city's drains and went away, still shaking their heads. Then one day came word from Tim; several words, be it said. ('It'.) His love was still true, he said, but he had transferred it to a South Sea Island girl. He enclosed his vest, because he had heard her father had fallen on 'Hard Times', by Dickens, racking his brains.

Down to the Quay Phoebe went and flung sock and vest far into the Tyne. From that day they stopped feeding the Quayside apprentices fresh salmon, and that should settle that controversy.

(PREBENDARY SULPHUR: "I don't follow this at all." BARRAS: "It's an apologue. Hence the inanimation." SULPHUR: "Of course, of course.")

Nearly

Almost resigned to the possibility that his expedition will never set out for Pattisbobo, Major Kalamity was not in the least surprised to learn that Leading Wren Angela Lurchabowte has failed to arrive in Spennymoor.

It appears that she descended from the train at Peterborough, and on being assured that this was not the nearest station for Spennymoor boarded the next one. During the next few days, she is understood to have got out and in at Grantham, Doncaster, York and Northallerton, pulling the communication cord as she deemed necessary.

Latest news is that on looking out at Gateshead, she pulled the cord for the final time and was carried, moaning distractedly, from the train. The Admiralty will not pay the £5 penalty unless British Railways render their account in triplicate. British Railways point out that they always render in quadruplicate. Lengthy litigation is expected.

No Tacks

SIR, – I find it strange that while you speak of old Frank Batterwick's early devotion to sock suspension you fail to mention that this had no connection with zumzumosophy. It is ximxomulism that treats of the theory that suspenders are unnecessary to keep up the human sock.

The arch-exponent of ximxomulism was Willie Kandelstick, who for years was to be seen walking about Sunderland with his socks slopping over his boots before he finally acquired the tranquillity of mind which enabled him to keep up his socks by sheer will power.

FREDA LAW-LUMMY, Sunderland.

No Bars

I have no comment to offer on the re-opened controversy about the British habit of going to the theatre apparently to drink. Most of the people I see in theatre bars are drinking more than apparently. Next time I make no comment, I shall try not to use 37 words on it.

Heaven knows I should be the last to complain about theatre drinkers who return late and stand on my feet; I have found feet to stand on all my life, even with areas like the Town Moor at my disposal. Besides, there is many another peril in the theatre. For years, a man has been following me about for the purpose of getting somewhere in the row behind me and giving his companions a running appreciation of the play.

When some character in Act One quotes from Shakespeare (which is what Act One is for), this man is saying breathlessly: "'...ripeness is all.' That's right!" – beating the actor to it by a short head. When the Archduke gets into a compromising situation, the voice behind elucidates: "Now Ferdinand – that's Sir Laurence – will come in. You watch!"

The fact that the next three characters to enter turn out to be the Rev. J. Oobattle, Big Chief Cow Catcher and a small brown dog abashes him not at all. He is probably convinced that Sir Laurence has taken the wrong turning backstage and is now running frantically up and down Grey Street.

And when Act Three's dénouement arrives, he utters a triumphant "Aah-haaaa!" He knew it all along.

I have never been able to pin this man down. Every time I turn my head to try to spot him, I meet a frosty stare from some quite innocent theatre-goer, accompanied by a "Tch, tch!" For the next three days, I keep going red up the back of my neck at the thought that I am just another theatre nuisance myself.

Mrs Chump

Why is it etiquette for a gentleman accompanying two ladies to walk between them? – CUTHBERT, Hexham.

To stop them coming to blows, you fool.

23

Beware of domesticity:
 Absent thee, oh young man!
 Absent thee from Felicity –
 And also Grace and Ann.

No?

"I cannot see the point of brewers' horse-drawn drays travelling through a tunnel and then returning by surface route to fetch the beer." With this clear shrill call, Mrs. Blookwith has again attacked Mr. Phil Thumpable's projected Longbenton–Backworth tunnel.

Mr. Thumpable has replied that the horses are not obliged to use the tunnel. "Is Mrs. Blookwith suggesting," he demands, "that horses should be forced to travel in tunnels against their will? Would Mrs. Blookwith like this if she were a horse?"

Brewing interests are now said to be envisaging a contretemps in which beer may be left stagnant in Longbenton.

'Stagnant in Longbenton' is of course the title of Mr. G.H. Elliott's latest novel. This is not Mr. G.H. Elliott, the soft-shoe shuffler. More litigation? Messrs. Gillifeather Hoote and Bunfroth Mennadgery, Q.C.s, live in hope.

An Old Story

Statisticians would get further with me (about 2.375 inches) if they would stop making decimals of the human body. One has just said that for every male in the United Kingdom there are 1.09 females. "This means," he adds, "that it is almost possible for every tenth man to have two wives."

"Almost," yes! Have you ever tried it, professor?

He also says that the expected lifespan of the British male is now 77 years, provided he gets up to 6^1/$_2$ (having avoided alcohol, I think it's fair to add).

Behind these cold figures there is surely an epic human story. Here is the British male, faced with all the hazards of the modern world (including the British female), and far from saying "What the hell?" and giving up, he and his kind are getting together in large numbers at 6^1/$_2$, shouting the slogan "On to 77, boys!"

At the same time, it should be pointed out that some old buffers, in their enthusiasm, are rather over-shooting the mark. It is not unknown for British males of 80 and even 90 to be seen around. Somebody should take these chaps aside and ask them what they think this is.

But the truly disturbing thing is that the British female 'can now expect to live 82 years'. There is an untidy overlap here. If the ladies are prepared to give a bit of ground, we might compromise on a nice round figure of eighty. I myself am willing to strain every nerve to this end.

Make it 82 and a bit. I feel like eighty already.

Up North

Mr. Egbald Knutt has enlisted Councillor Mrs. Wallop in an effort to teach 'Geordie' to General Damgud-Fellah, one of the 47 claimants to the Northumbrian throne. Mrs. Wallop contends that the word 'hyem' (as in 'gannin' hyem') is of Norse origin. Homeward-bound Norsemen, she believes, were the origin of the expression, 'leading a Norse to water'.

This is barmy, Mr. Knutt states (as who wouldn't?). He quotes the mediaeval Welsh bard Cadwatter as being the first exponent of the word, which suggests that it is Erse rather than Norse.

"I've seen many a Norse leading an Erse," comments a well-known undertaker.

Probably, Yes

SIR, – Mr. Sam Bamboozle's scheme for making horses run backwards would, so far from facilitating the start of races, make it even more hazardous. Does Mr. Bamboozle not know that horses are thickest at the back end? How then, with an exceptionally big field, could all the horses be got backwards to the tapes at once?

A better plan would be to have alternate horses facing different ways. They would all fit in perfectly, as in joinerwork.

Are the Carlisle Bamboozles related to the Workington Hoodwinks?

J.G. SPOOF, Darlington.

Ah, Youth!

I recall another of my expeditions with dear old Glook and Crumble, when we went in search of antiquated folk tunes, which were to be found, you may wager, among some pretty antiquated folk. Off we set, with Glook bending his steps northward and Crumble walking behind, straightening them out.

Crumble laughingly said we might find a moorland aria in the moorland area, and wasn't it lucky we had brought our ancient banjo? Indeed it was, for I laughingly fetched him a good clout with it.

One morning early, as we stood close in the shadow of the Cheviot (it was Shadowday early closing), we came on an old man singing inaudibly to a stringless melodion, something we had never heard before, nor will again, until the sun sets on all our days in a blaze of euphonious twaddle.

It was a tender song of lost love, telling of how an old man and his old woman lived for 73 years by the Till – till he vanished. (Oh, well.) She rose one morning and he had gone. Out on the moors she ran, calling, and barking her shins, and calling some more. But he had vanished forever. Three weeks later, a postcard arrived, saying he was in Bournemouth, and just try to get him back!

That's the way the song went, my friends, and no! – we made no attempt to stop it.

Knee Sense

Miss Alberta McSopp of North Shields, ranked Number Three in the Vital Statistic of the North-East contest, who has alleged that the right knee of Miss Gwendoline Goggling, the winner, is three-quarters of an inch larger than her left, has in turn been accused by Miss Julietta Foist, Newbiggin (Number Five), of padding both of her knees.

"Any girl who would wear falsies to enhance her knee beauty is beneath contempt," states Miss Foist.

Miss Adelina Nottarf, principal runner-up, is considering action against the Jarrow judge who voted against her on the grounds that her knees were 'too starkly provocative'.

Mrs. Chump

Why is it etiquette for a gentleman to precede a lady upstairs? – CUTHBERT, Hexham.

So that if he trips, he will have something soft to fall on. You keep asking questions, don't you?

At Last

I shall now give you give you some further thoughts on the provenance of zumzumosophy, because I want you to know that my apprehensions come in crowds and I dread the rustling of the grass.

Old Frank Batterwick was more than the theorist who pronounced that the human trouser could support life with its turnup supplanted by a turn-down. He also understood humanity's foibles and frequently asked: Where is it now, the glory and the dream?

Frank had long studied the kind of man who, in walking down a crowded street, suddenly becomes aware that his trouser turnup has turned down. Such a man invariably casts furtive glances about him, halts, stands on one leg and, with a pitiable attempt at nonchalance, adjusts the wretched turnup.

Old Frank had crept up on many such men and had found that, with barely an exception, they braved out this spurious nonchalance by humming self-consciously: "Zum, zumm, zummm." Hence, when he gave his discovery to the world, he had no hesitation in calling it the quantum theory.

(PREBENDARY SULPHUR: "Why these unacknowledged quotations from Wordsworth?" BARRAS: "Did Wordsworth ever acknowledge me?" SULPHUR: "Yes. In 'Liberty', Line 73." BARRAS: "Oh.")

Signal Failure

Major Kalamity has now been interviewed by Commander Badstuff. "I require to know," the commander began, "how it is alleged that you are 205 years of age."

"Because I am a Ukrainian peasant named Mrs. Boris O'Brien," replied the major, "and I charge you with being in love with gorgeous Wren Lurchabowte."

The commander blushed but produced, out of a hat, Professor Beetroot's landlady, Mrs. Allthumbs, to swear that the major was born in 1903. "I was his mother for a time," she said. This was a sensation as well as a lie.

Leading Wren Angela will report back that if Major Kalamity is Admiral Shimmering-Dulally, he is feigning loss of memory to cover the fraudulent drawing of £134,785 in half-pension. If he is not the admiral – and even if he is, hang it – anybody is entitled to ask the meaning of this. I say only that strange fits of passion have I known.

Shame!

SIR, – If there is some advantage in having jockeys facing behind them, as in the Boat Race, surely you don't have to have the horses running backwards in order to achieve this? You would get the same effect if the jockey simply sat and faced the horse's tail while the horse ran forward.

To make horses run backwards is unspeakable. Does Mr. Sam Bamboozle not know that their legs bend the wrong way for this? Do not interfere with nature! They were given tails, were they not, to keep flies off?

CELIA DUNCH, Ponteland.

An Old Suit

About a year ago, as the time flies, this column spoke of the lobster-rich Archipelagos of Les Minquiers et Les Ecrehos. What happened, I ask, except that my typewriter broke down under the strain? Well, the matter refuses to die and I have been asked, by my creditors, to write again on the subject, at three-halfpence a line.

The Archipelagos of Les Minquiers at Les Ecrehos (sole agent Jack Drubbit, W.1) were awarded to Britain by the International Court in a series of sessions which might well be described as sensational, whether they were or not. Putting the case for Belgium was Maître d'Otelle. A stout job he was making of it when the judges stopped the proceedings on the 15th day and pointed out that Belgium wasn't in this at all and the whole thing was between Britain and France.

M. d'Otelle had another look at his brief and acknowledged jovially that the laugh was on him all right; he had thought he was defending Jacques Pustule, a man back home who was accused of murdering 17 wives, including some of his own. A sporting lot, the judges saw the joke in time, and after they had passed it along to each other got down to business again.

"Where were we?" asked a rather famous Scandinavian jurist.

"Almost certainly not," replied the Greek advocate in Italian, showing off.

And so international understanding bred international equity and 94 days later the Archipelagos of Les Minquiers et Les Ecrehos were awarded to Britain, with custody of the lobsters. The world acclaimed a jurisdictional triumph, all except Jacques Pustule who, let down by the absence of the Maître, was found damnably guilty. "A bas le justice!" he cried, and shot the jury. Justice was always unmultiplicable.

Kid Stuff

Madam! Is your husband handy about the house? When you ask him to warm the copper, does he go out and set fire to a policeman? And what about the baby? Does your husband know what to bath the baby in, apart from a copper bath? Or does he think a copper bath is a constabulary shower?

Tell your husband to bath the baby in WHOOSH. Only after a WHOOSH bath does the baby come out shiny and new. Or does he think a constabulary shower is an unpleasant superintendent? And does he know what to do with the old baby?

The answer is – WHOOSH! Tell your husband nothing is half as good as WHOOSH, and WHOOSH is twice as good as nothing. How did all this copper stuff get in here? What is this – a police convention? Is a police convention the age-old preservation of law?

Tell your husband to use WHOOSH! And don't throw out the age-old preservation with the bath-water. WHOOSH!

Shelve This

'Russia As I Saw It', by A. Husky Carpenter (Pyngpong and Urtch, 25s.).

En route for Russia, Mr. Carpenter lost his way in South Shields. South Shields is not Russia, of course, and the letters 'v', 'q', 'e' and 'l' were stolen from his typewriter. On reflection, he would have done well to have changed the title and avoided the word 'equivalent'.

Had you chanced to be on Wallsend High Street on June 10th, 1732, you would have seen an ugly old man, always assuming he was there, and not in the Coach and Horses again. You would also be 224 years old today. Many happy returns! If I have used this opening before, many happy returns to it too.

(PREBENDARY SULPHUR: "Eleven times at the latest count." BARRAS: "Hats off for the late count!" SULPHUR: "That too.")

At second glance (eschewing the first), you would have noticed that the cloak he wore, though shabby, was that of a gentleman; the gentleman had come back before he could get the hat. At third glance, he might well have asked you who the hell you thought you were, staring like that.

This man was proud old Ena Zinc, last of his race. His late twin sister James had been second last. The whole family were rotten runners. As he stood there, wondering if the parson had been drunk at their christening...

(PREBENDARY SULPHUR: "Where is the rest of this story?" BARRAS: "I have gone into the Coach and Horses again.")

The Nth?

SIR, – Your explanation of how zumzumosophy got its name is laughable to a degree. May I set out the facts?

As a lifelong student of the human trouser in all its vicissitudes, though admittedly especially in relation to its turnup, old Frank Batterwick well knew that one of the most incorrigible of mankind's habits was its twanging, during moments of stress, of its braces.

Everybody knows that this produces a 'zumzum' kind of noise. I hope this ends this controversy for good if not for all.

FREDA LAW-LUMMY, Sunderland.

Well, What?

Mrs. Blookwith has now claimed that her alleged cruelty in suggesting that brewers' horses might be compelled to go through the Longbenton-Backworth tunnel is far outdone by that of Mr. Phil Thumpable himself. "What could be more cruel," she asks, "than to require a horse to return for a load of beer after he has already been through a tunnel without it?"

"Contemplation of a suppositional horse," states Mr. Thumpable, "proceeding with conjectural beer in a theoretical dray through a hypothetical tunnel leads me to suppose that Mrs. Blookwith is herself a mere postulation."

No Singing?

How eagerly I plunged into an article on 'Conversations With Wild Creatures', for I have always wanted to know how to talk to women at dinner, but the whole thing turned out to mean what it said, unlike me talking to women at dinner.

Apparently you can communicate with any dumb animal 'by approaching and blowing up and down your nose'. The animal responds by blowing up and down *his* nose and 'in no time at all, he will be eating off your hand'. Now it gets credible.

I have always considered that journalists should think twice about some of the material they write. (On reflection, I'd be happy if they thought once.) The trouble with confronting the newspaper-reading public with details of how to do something is that it is liable to haul off and egg its friends on to do it.

Any doctor will tell you, while striking you casually on the knee, that a physician has only to bruit it around that the remedy for the Common Cold – better known as the Reciprocity of Duties Bill, 1823 – is to drink tepid tea strained over rusty saws and presently the whole nation will be doing something not very much like that, having got it wrong.

Now that we have been instructed on how to talk to animals, and assuming we get it right (in which case, there goes my logic), the country's animal population will spend the next few months backing away from snorting citizens.

I should report, however, that I for one have been unable to work the system. (It must be infallible.) The other day, I met a horse who was gazing, as horses do, across a hedge. I breathed heavily into his nostrils, after looking both ways. He made no reply.

Perhaps both of us had a Common Cold and ought to have struck each other's knees.

Up North

Once again, Mr. Egbald Knutt is quoting the ancient Welsh bard Cadwatter to support him in an etymological imbroglio. It seems that even the substantive 'hinny' is not a truly Geordie word, for Cadwatter 700 years ago wrote a Welsh poem (in Urdu) in which he used the word to describe mules and women.

He was travelling through Northumbria at the time, playing his harp to the barons to earn his keep. "It was a baron enterprise," as he wryly remarked, but he certainly got his keep. It was the keep of Alnwick Castle. He deserved it after that 'baron' stuff, historians believe.

Kapital Crime

"Dialectical materialist and elderly mother require housekeeper." – *Not small enough to be unnoticed (by me) ad.*

> *When she shifted the stains from the sideboard,*
> *We nodded and said, "That's the stuff!"*
> *Then she shifted the bloom from the wardrobe*
> *And we just couldn't praise her enough.*
> *We thought we'd discovered a treasure,*
> *But now she'd be better off dead,*
> *For she shifted the Marx from the bookcase –*
> *And then we just had to see Red.*

Mrs. Chump

When acknowledging a lady's greeting, should a gentleman bow or raise his bowler hat? – *BERT, Stockton.*

He should certainly raise his bowler hat, Bert, unless he is wearing a trilby! (Ho-ho. may I say?).

The correct procedure is both to bow *and* raise the hat. He should, however, avoid bowing so low that the hat drops off – unless, of course, the lady has bowed so low that *her* hat has dropped off, just as you might put your elbows in your jelly to avoid embarrassing a guest.

Yes

Packs of dogs, I read, are howling at the moon in a North-East seaside resort. Is this known as the Whitley Bay?

Elderly readers rest here.

26

And now I see that a man who broke into a shop and stole his own teeth, which he had left earlier for repair, found himself charged – though not with false pretences.

Asked if he had anything to say, the toothless man replied, "Mish twashlish frosh wush."

"What language is that – gum Arabic?" asked the magistrate amid loud laughter (his own).

I well recall, from my reporting days on the Northern circuit ("Circuit and see," said my editor amid loud laughter – mine), that in the case of Strahdottle versus Alf Duster (the Zimzam Hot Dog Trust intervening), it was held by Mr. Justice Eckond that a man tickling the middle of his back with a false beard put on the wrong way round while sunbathing is not liable, unless the incident takes place on a Sunday, in which event it might be classed as a theatrical performance.

The case was lost, and hasn't been found to this day.

Beered

The team of engineering students which, under Dr. Finicky, has been in Ashington examining Mrs. Wibduck's bird bath, is now back in Leadgate University, sullen and baffled. Theoretically, it is impossible for Professor Beetroot to fall into the bath, as it stands four feet high and is only 15 inches across. "No fully grown man could do it," states Dr. Finicky, "although a fully grown infant might."

The students used a cardboard model filled with beer for the tests and exception to this has been taken by Miss Avril Sleet. "Birds do not make a practice of bathing in beer," she said yesterday or last November or some damned time, "whatever the habits of university students."

None At All

SIR, – We seem to have come a long way from Mr. Sam Bamboozle's original plan to make horses run backwards. This, I suspect, would require two jockeys to each horse and neither would be able to see, because they would be looking straight at each other.

And what purpose will the backward-looking jockey serve, except to see what is coming up behind? It is true that Boat Race crews face backwards, but at least they are pulling oars to help things along. What is the good of that to a horse?

THOMAS FATT-FATT, Newbiggin.

Bell Cracks

I have been looking very closely – because these old eyes grow ever more tired – into the recently revived interest in the Brontë: quartet, and I have decided that they never even existed! (My exclamation mark.)

They were works of fiction, every one of them, as anyone with half an eye, albeit young and fresh, could see. Three weird sisters and a dissolute brother – what else could these be except characters from the alleged novels of Acton, Currer and Ellis Bell? (My question mark, too.)

And there's another thing (there – a shade to the left). Everybody knows that Branwell Brontë: was a railway clerk, but has anybody ever suggested that he wrote Bradshaw's Guide under the pseudonym 'Brighton Bell'? Well, then. The truth is that they were all invented by the rich imagination of old Patrick Brontë:, who was the only real person in the Haworth ménage.

When Charlotte came to him and said, "Father, I am having a novel published," he replied, "My dear, that will cost you a lot." You see? He couldn't conceive that anybody would give good money to publish it. I know this stamps him as a credible human being because people are always saying to me, "How much do you pay newspapers to publish your rubbish?"

Oh, Patrick *was* Charlotte, which accounts for her peculiar behaviour when she visited Mrs. Gaskell, who was expecting somebody of four feet eleven without sidewhiskers. Does this also explain why Emily was unhappy in Brussels? Of course! How? I'm working on that! Meanwhile, I have to send out for more exclamation marks.

The old man achieved all this deception because he cunningly built up a reputation for forgetfulness. Thus, when people called and asked for Anne, he would back absently away, go upstairs and discharge a volley out of a bedroom window. Nobody would call again after that.

Except Mrs. Gaskell. She persisted in writing 'The Life of Charlotte (née Patrick) Brontë:'. He took a potshot at her, but hit Branwell, who was, as we know, himself. None of the family was ever the same again.

He Was There!

An amazing piece of good luck has come the way of Major Kalamity. He has been able to engage for the ketch Imbendin a new skipper who is reputed to know where Pattisbobo is. This oracle is old Joe Weskit, who claims to have touched Pattisbobo in 1897, the same year in which he touched the Banana Isles, Reykjavik and Second Mate Alf Crikey.

An expert on transmigration, Skipper Weskit has a theory that the early settlers in Seaton Sluice got there by sitting on rafts at Whitley Bay and allowing themselves to be tugged along by the currents. This, of course, runs counter to the contention of middle-aged Mrs. Guss, who holds that they could have done it just as easily by running along the Blyth road. Rather more easily, her neighbour Mrs. Brown thinks.

"How did anybody called Brown get into this man's column?" asks Prebendary Sulphur.

Up Howdon!

The news that the Fulham gasometer is listed as an ancient monument has gone down well in Howdon, but the Howdon gasometer keeps on going up. It will never have any kind of list, say the proud natives, who point to Mrs. Dimwitty as their only ancient monument.

> There's a broken old man down in Howdon
>   And he wanders alone by the docks.
> In his youth he loved Mrs. Dimwitty,
>   Who was fifteen stone three in her socks.
> But along came some grim-faced officials,
>   And to them may be traced his sad plight,
> For they pulled down his love and erected
>   The gasometer bang on the site.

If it comes to that, what about the lady who said to a London bus conductor, "Is this a Tooting bus?"

"Only in traffic jams," was the polite reply.

She was a Barking lady, as it happened, and had to be carried in somebody's lap.

Hickory Dickory

A problem which has perplexed me ever since, as a child, I first got on to my feet and began walking into the furniture, concerns the old nursery rhyme about the three men in the tub. Eventually I shall get around to being perplexed at still walking into the furniture.

This rhyme begins, I have always understood, "With a rubber dub-dub, / Three men in a tub..." The thing that has puzzled me is: What is a rubber dub-dub? What, if it comes to that, is any kind of dub-dub, and why did the men have to have a rubber one, given their respective trades?

My own juvenile theory was that the rubber dub-dub was an object used by the men to plug a hole, either in a candlestick or a pound of mince, and the baker was there only to make the numbers up. I held tenaciously to this even after a larger boy assured me that this was a 'bung'. There couldn't possibly be such a word as 'bung,' I felt. I remember laughing scornfully in the larger boy's face. I don't remember much else.

It was only recently that I chanced to be curled up with my small niece's nursery rhyme book, the TV having gone off, and there I saw the phrase "With a rub-a-dub-dub..." To say I laughed uproariously is but a poor way to describe my reaction to this pathetic misprint. I have said it now, though. At once, I called my small niece to have a look at it. "That is the correct spelling," she said coldly, "and can't we have some peace around here?"

It's a dreadful experience to have one's illusions fractured. My back hurt too when I tried to uncurl myself. Then I remembered my propensity for getting songs all wrong. For countless years I kept singing 'Smiling Through' to the tune of the 'William Tell' overture and wondering why it sounded like neither. I shall find myself a dishonourable grave.

No matter. I intend to go on thinking in terms of a 'rubber-dub-dub'. A man who is not free to walk into the furniture is not free at all.

Nark It

"A small printer ordered a policeman out." – *The Baden-Baden Echo.*

> *The bobby aroused all the small printer's devil,*
> *And his story was printed in letters of flame;*
> *He was never the sort to be frightened of coppers,*
> *Though he wasn't the size of sixpenn'orth of same.*

They Couldn't

SIR, – The implication of correspondence initiated by Mr. Sam Bamboozle appears to be that Boat Race crews may be asked to do the impossible. How can eight men get into a bottomless craft and run along the bed of the river? I suppose Oxbridge chaps, who are the flower of our youth, might just manage this. But backwards? And what about the cox? How could his little legs keep up with the rest?

GRETA FLOUNDERING, Haltwhistle.

Are You Human?

Are you breathing? Do your feet hurt when you meet a duchess? What is that on the end of your nose? Answer (a), (b) or (c) to the following questions and then turn to Page 87 of the 'Bricklayer's Financial Times' to find out why you should not be shot.

1. Your elderly Auntie Kate is sitting out on the window-sill cleaning one of those old-fashioned sash windows when it glides gently down and traps her legs. Do you (a) send for a window-cleaner to finish the job? (b) make proper arrangements to have her back scratched now and then? (c) hook the blind to her suspenders when it gets dark?
2. You hear two girls discussing a third party. Do you (a) get annoyed because you weren't invited to the first two parties? (b) send for the Fire Brigade? (c) take out fire insurance? (d) or third party insurance?
3. A man in a restaurant hangs his coat on your wife's ear. Do you (a) hang your hat on her other ear? (b) stuff your gloves in her mouth? (c) ask her what she is standing there for anyway? (d) apologise? (e) Why? What have *you* done? (f) Nothing, but anything for a quiet life.
4. Do you think there are too many questions in that last group?
5. Your best friend is wearing a county cap. Do you (a) not think this is hardly the outfit for a girl? (b) make arrangements to have your back scratched now and then? (c) consider the whole thing ridiculous?

If you have answered (a) to each of the above questions, who do you think you are? If you have answered (z) you cannot have read them properly. If you have been asleep, all right, all right.

The Secret

What is it about WHOOSH that makes it so different from all the other exoguble emolugobes? Many of these products contain bromoskilkin, zefugim, woowoo, helobrixtoplactimus and fut, all of which are guaranteed to make your washing whiter, brighter, lighter and slighter.

Why is it that WHOOSH does none of these things? Why is it that WHOOSH makes your dirty washing dirtier? The answer is – WHOOSH contains muck! Soak your weekly wash in WHOOSH and it will come out filthy.

Mrs. Chump

When arranging a bridge dinner, is it advisable to have high stakes? – AMELIA, Stocksfield.

I take it that when you speak of 'stakes', my dear, you mean 'steaks'. I certainly do not think it desirable to have the steaks too high, unless curried.

In any case, I do feel a bridge is an odd place to give a dinner.

28

E asily the most enjoyable headlines of the week were "Election Slide In Iceland" and "Mrs. Braddock Holds Up House".

A good funny man can do something with such material, one feels, and proceeds to the usual rot.

Hard Blow

It was in 1927 or 1894 that old Joe Weskit, newly-appointed skipper of the ketch Imbendin, performed his experiments to prove that the early native settlers in Seaton Sluice were blown there on rafts from Whitley Bay. Shoving off 82 times on a raft from Whitley Bay, he was blown to sea 74 times. He was dragged in again 63 times, struggling bitterly, by a man called Junk.

"I got sick of rescuing him," Junk reported.

On the eleven occasions that Junk was at home with a chill, old Joe, unhampered, found himself blown back to Whitley Bay, thus proving that the early native settlers in Whitley Bay were blown there on rafts from Sheffield.

(PREBENDARY SULPHUR: "Sheffield?" BARRAS: "That is where the rafts were made." SULPHUR: "Naturally.")

Mrs. Chump

At dinner, ought one to wave one's napkin about? – JOHN, Walbottle.

No, John. If you wish to attract the attention of the gentleman opposite, lob a bun in his direction. If you are merely emphasising some conversational point, stab at your food with your fork. The purpose of your napkin in this case is to wipe the gravy off the lady next to you.

Feathered Tales

There are not many things I remember about my childhood, although I'm pretty sure I did have one. One thing I recall, however, in addition to a tendency to try to wear my glasses upside-down, is that I must have been a trusting little chap, because I believed anything anybody told me.

Jovial playmates of mine had only to bring the news that the entire city of Newcastle was on fire for me to rush out into the street and pelt off to see the blaze. Somebody else had to rush after me to point me in the right direction.

One of the mistaken boyish beliefs I cherished was that parrots could talk. I was never, of course, foolish enough to suppose that you could hold a conversation with a parrot, and indeed I reserved my confidences for an old horse. But parrotophiles have always claimed that if you stand in front of a parrot saying "Bless my soul" often enough, he will get the idea eventually.

So he will, but it is not what you would call talking. Well, it is not what I would call talking. Many parrot owners (up to three) have invited me to hear their parrots saying "Mary had a little lamb" or "I'm Pretty Polly, and I don't like it much because I'm a male parrot." That is not what I want.

What I want is to come on a parrot unintroduced and try to guess what the devil he is talking about. Slow starter though I was, I was able by the age of 13 to say "Humpty Dumpty sat on a wall" with considerably more clarity than a parrot of my acquaintance who was reputed to be 113.

As for budgerigars, which seem to be replacing potted geraniums in most homes these days, I would even back the discredited parrot to beat any budgie in the talking stakes by not less than a long beak. If a budgie brought me the news that Newcastle was on fire, I would sit right there where I was, uncomprehending.

In fact, if I couldn't talk better than a budgerigar, I would give the idea up and concentrate on spreading psittacosis. Find out what you're good at and stick to it, is what I say.

Joint Action

In the great Miss Vital Statistic battle, Miss McSopp has now answered Miss Foist's accusation that she wore falsies on her knees by alleging that Miss Foist wore flesh-coloured skintight garters under her kneecaps "in order to obtain uplift." Miss Foist has now further alleged that Miss Nottarf dabbed make-up on her knees to disguise the wrinkles.

Miss Gwendoline Goggling, the precarious Miss Vital Statistic herself, has been accused by Miss Nottarf of being afraid to stand too close to the judges in case they heard 'the deafening creaking' of her knees.

No Such Word

"You can't blow a hunting horn with false teeth." – A Master of Foxhounds.
Among other things you can't do are:

a. Knock the top off a boiled egg with a ball of wool.
b. Ride a bicycle sidesaddle.
c. Sew buttons on to cast steel kneepads.
d. Run a mile in four minutes. (Well, I can't.)

89

Another feat you can't perform with false teeth is play blow football. You can, of course, leave them in the dressing room, or request your girl friend to keep them for you in her handbag along with your wooden leg, but you must ask yourself whether she will still want to marry you, or indeed whether she has an exceptionally large handbag. If so, she might be able to accommodate your wig as well. Incidentally, good luck on your honeymoon.

Among musical instruments you *can* play with false teeth are the bones and the ukulele, but not simultaneously, unless you take your boots off. Anyway, a hunting horn is not a musical instrument within the meaning of any act known to Mr. Gilliefeather Hoote, Q.C., although he concedes that eating a water melon is difficult for men with false teeth or large ears (Bandlegloff versus Blotchy, 1934).

A false-toothed Master of Foxhounds of my acquaintance couldn't lead the dancing off at the hunt ball, but only because his partner was drunk.

Finally

Here are some answers to correspondents:

Mrs. K., Burnopfield: Sorry, I've forgotten.
Stan, Birtley: (a) Yes, (b) Yes, (c) Yes, (d) Yes, (e) Probably, (f) Quite probably, (g) Almost certainly.
Willie, Ron, Tubby, Dave, Old Grubmug, Bedlington: What?

Jenny kissed me when we met,
Jumping from her horsehair seat.
Time, you thief, a kiss I get
From the horse would be more sweet.

Some Bird

Science may have proved it impossible for Professor Beetroot to fall into Mrs. Wibduck's bird bath, but he did so again 13 times last week.

Dr. Finicky, the Leadgate University statistician, fresh from computing the number of ginger-haired Consett gasmen with old bicycles, yesterday measured Mrs. Wibduck's garden with chalk and tape measure. Afterwards, he concealed himself in a laurel bush with a disgruntled blackbird while the professor and Mrs. Wibduck took a stroll.

The only result was that the professor skidded on a bit of Dr. Finicky's chalk and fell into Mrs. Wibduck's arms. "Now isn't that better than a bird bath, you old silly billy?" the lady was heard to chuckle.

Bison Blues

SIR, – Who is this Mr. Alfred Zimbo who claims that Mrs. Laglumb fell over a bison in Crawcrook? There are no bison in Crawcrook. The incident took place in Corbridge.

Turning the corner of Coostoppit Street, Mrs. Laglumb came face to face with the animal. They both backed and snorted. Mrs. Laglumb's hat then fell off and it was in trying to retrieve it that she went headlong over the beast.

The bison, I have been given to understand, took it in good part.

BERTRAM YIPPT, Darlington.

(PREBENDARY SULPHUR: Who *are* this Alfred Zimbo and Mrs. Laglumb?" BARRAS: "They dropped in last week, unnoticed." SULPHUR: "It's that hole in the ceiling." BARRAS: "I don't understand you.")

Auto Suggestions

A disturbing fact has come to my notice concerning automation. It's that I don't know what the devil it is.

As I see it, it will not be many years before all the work in the world which is at present done by machines will be done by other machines. There will be a vast accumulation of redundant mechanism, and something will have to be done about it. It might even have to be done by people. It is either that or set to and try to find something for all those machines to do with their extra leisure.

The modern machine is pretty enlightened, and nobody expects him to start acting like the Luddites and getting himself organised into gangs, muttering: "Let's smash these new-fangled monsters." At the same time, no machine likes to stand on a street corner, smoking cigarette ends, when he knows he has still a few well-oiled years left in him.

After all, it is not so long since these same machines as are now being written off were hailed as being able to work out in ten seconds calculations which an expensively trained physicist would spend 18 months over, without sleep. Moreover, they were less likely to leave the answers on restaurant table-cloths. And how many machines have defected through the Iron Curtain? There is no 'Third Machine', is there?

No, we owe it to these faithful servants to find them happy pursuits in their new-found leisure – the joy of gardening, for instance, or wall-papering, or pottering about on a roof, sticking on loose tiles.

In fact, if any machine reads this, I for one can put him in the way of filling in all his leisure time for years to come.

Draw The Line

"A schoolmistress said at Ilford County Court that she did not like seeing men's short underwear on a clothes-line." – *The Washing Post.*

> *Though poets sing that woman's tender sighs*
> *Bring tears unbidden to a strong man's eyes,*
> *My lady's eyes eschew the second glance*
> *When she's confronted by a fellow's pants.*

Cagey

Mrs. Chump writes: A very good way to make a wickerwork snood for an ironing board is first of all to mark out the dimensions of an old pair of braces on the inside of a plastic mackintosh. This is advisable in case rain descends before the job is done.

Some people favour wire mesh for the snood rather than wickerwork, but this sometimes tends to rust when it comes in contact with stout. Wickerwork, on the other hand, is inclined to drop off when the ironing board is tucked under the stairs of buses on long journeys, or even short ones. To counteract this, you should tack the snood on, though this entails considerable extra labour every time the board is to be used.

Tacking is inadvisable if the board is made of indiarubber. Indiarubber ironing boards are seldom very serviceable, however. Neither, of course, are braces when it rains.

Up North

Mr. Egbald Knutt is convinced that the entire Geordie language stems from the ballads of Cadwatter, the ancient Welsh bard. It is said, he says, and is saying it, that one day Cadwatter sang before red-haired Harry Hotspur, not knowing that red-haired Harry wanted to sing first.

The song was the old Welsh air, 'Yy ffyddldi dyddl' ('Ginger, You're Barmy!'), and as the tender strains smote his ears Hotspur rushed out and took to his horse, though what he took to it we shall never know, as I have spent ten minutes over this bit and am having what I say, and am saying it, is a creative blockage.

Contains Muck

Laboratory tests, carried out in laboratories, have proved conclusively that scientists, carrying out tests (scientific ones, in laboratories) on WHOOSH, have in 57,867 cases finished with their aprons filthy. Why? WHOOSH contains muck! Try the acid test. Chuck acid over your nightie and watch it disappear. Would you like to smother your grandfather? Smother him in WHOOSH and he will come out disgusting.

Autumn Book

'A Book of Zysspprremian Verse', translated by Alf Backover (Waggle, 10s.6d).

This may not be a book for all who have sought a translation of Zysspprremian verse, but it is undeniably a book. Mr. Backover has perhaps not perfectly caught the nuances of 'Xycht fru Mivd', but none can quarrel with his rendering of 'Klinnby vij Oooooo!' as 'Pardon?'

30

The North-Eastern Electricity Board's decision to issue turnupless trousers to its meter-readers prompts five questions: (a) Has that majestic body come round to the views of old Frank Batterwick?; and (b) Is this column being overhauled by bureaucracy?

Is the Board prepared to go the whole hog? It claims that the trouser turnup 'collects dirt and frequently causes people to trip and fall downstairs'. Does it, however, support the Batterwick contention that the prime reason for the abolition of the turnup is that it presents perpetual opportunity for the feminine remark, 'Your trouser turnup is turned down'? Will it offer to issue trousers with turndown tops? (Told you there were five.)

It is true that some housewives do not like to see their meter-readers falling downstairs. The housewife is sporadically kindly. At the same time, a meter-reader with the frayed edges of his trousers bound with old electrician's tape is not a prepossessing sight for the jaded suburban chatelaine.

The North Eastern Electricity Board will have to think again. Even such a historic institution, with its proud claim to have fostered the ampere on which the sun never sets, is not above being told to take a running jump unless it embraces ximxomulism. Or is it zumzumosophy? I don't remember, having just fallen downstairs.

Lost Again

Where is Pattisbobo? Commander Badstuff has surfaced with the news that in 1842 Britain concluded a treaty with the Hobnob of Bakkijooss under which Pattisbobo was to receive the Empire's entire production of hoghides as recompense for relinquishing all claim to the sovereignty of St. Petersburg, which was not, of course, Britain's to negotiate.

Whitehall sources say that this seems to prove, or appears to seem to prove, or if not to prove, at least to suggest to hint at, the possibility that Pattisbobo's whereabouts are not unknown.

Major Kalamity is grateful for this firm intelligence.

Travellers' Checks

I am not a pessimistic man by nature. It is long practice that has got me like that.

I must say, however, that when I keep reading of plans to build gigantic

94

new bus stations in Newcastle I feel like joining a deputation to the City Council. Well, not exactly joining it, but walking along thirty yards behind it as it goes into the Town Hall.

I have nothing against buses as such (and such I am pretty sure is what they are). I can even, after all these years, travel standing up in one without lurching against all the other standing passengers and starting one of those involuntary stampedes down the gangway.

But if we are going to have huge bus stations for the buses to drive into, what I want to know is this: Who is going to see that people like me (and frankly I mean me) find their way out of the stations and back into the stream of life again?

I have enough trouble in railway stations. Deposited in the middle of one, surrounded by miles of track and with a choice of several bridges to cross, I usually end up at the top of a small staircase in a cabin full of levers.

Nor is the size of the station really relevant. I have been known, in a tiny country station, to stand waiting for a train on the wrong side of a one-way track, all the while wondering why there was no platform on my side. If we are going to have the same trouble with bus stations, I might just as well stay at home. I can get lost quite easily there if I put my mind to it.

What, I ask, was wrong with the good old days? Even I, when I saw a pole on the pavement marked 'Bus Stop,' had a pretty good idea what it was.

Still, it took 120 years, historians tell me, to complete St. Nicholas's Cathedral, and they were pretty fast workers in those days. Assuming that sort of scale for erecting bus stations, I've got time to die in dignity at the age of 97, falling off my bicycle.

Up North

A document which has come to light in Jarrow, as far as that is possible, is believed to be the work of Dekrepit, an eccentric chronicler who was writing his chrinocles (he was a rotten typist) at about the time when Cadwatter, the ancient Welsh ballad-monger, was singing his ditties up and down the Tyne, to the accompaniment of wet feet.

Dekrepit describes how Cadwatter arrived to sing to King Isnibs, who was holding court at Howdon – with one arm, as his other arm was holding Queen Briskit. "Greetings, King Baldcoot..." Cadwatter began.

"That was last week!" shouted Isnibs. *"I'm king now!"*

Cadwatter then sang 'Any Old Iron', because it wasn't only ballads that he monged. He also monged iron and fish. He was a versatile monger.

"That must be the flattest iron in Howdon," observed Queen Briskit. "Why don't you mong a versatile?"

But Cadwatter decided to leave it at that, and having left it, left. Dekrepit says he became a rumour-monger, but that may be a canard.

Controversy

SIR, – There seems to be some concern that a horse should not wear cold leather next to his skin, but what about cinema organists? Many horses are quite happy to wear woolly jerkins, but I can point to numerous cinema organists who would find them itchy.

The horse is a beast.

BERTIE PLOPP, Consett.

(PREBENDARY SULPHUR: "How did this unannounced stuff get in? Is there another hole?" BARRAS: "I am being overhauled by bureaucracy." SULPHUR: "What has that to do with it?" BARRAS: "Nothing, and the next item is waiting.")

Mrs. Chump

I read in the paper that I could carry stout in my upturned hat. Does this hold good? – Dinah, Blyth.

Surely you mean does this hold well, my dear? You must watch your grammar. The answer is yes, if it is a stout hat.

It is one of the joys of writing this column, or would be if there were any, that it pleases nobody. I do not welcome, therefore, the harmonious intrusion from Miss Sybil Spritely, of Heaton, who says that her cat, her dog, her rabbit and her Uncle Jim snore happily over my work every Sunday.

What 'Anarchist' of Wallsend demands, however, is a *Family Through My Hat,* reflecting 'all the unsavoury animosities of that monstrous institution'. I keep trying.

A Treat

'Brutality, bestiality and fiendish horror'. This is how L.J. Taptoe describes everyday life in East Boldon. Mr. Taptoe is the fairly unknown author turned hod-carrier whose timely exposé is only one of the attractions to be featured here shortly. Others include:

'Every Night a Purple Eye', the full story of husband-bashing by Tantobie women.

'Sex in Ashington – Where the Hell is It?' by Maisie Ooguggle, housewife.

'Razor Blades in My Bumpers'. A Wallsend Teddy Boy talks, almost literately.

'My Contorted Addiction'. Confessions of a Hebburn toenail-biter.

Well Bread

"The English race was not made on foreign white flour." – Letter in the *Myopic Observer.*

> *The flour of England's manhood's rising still.*
> *And one who's mealy-mouthed is not yet born;*
> *While strong men yet go through the English mill*
> *They'll come out whiter than the alien corn.*

Dry Rot

It may or may not – and nobody is going to knock me down for saying that – be significant that Ashington this year had its driest spring in the living memory of a rather young person. There are those who attribute this to Professor Beetroot's rain-mopping experiments, although he is alleged by others to have spent more time falling into the bird bath of his hostess, Mrs. Wibduck.

"The bath, already depleted by drought," states Miss Avril Sleet, "can ill afford to be further mopped up by the incursions of this irresponsible crank's whiskers."

The whiskers continue to attract controversy. The professor yesterday visited an inept barber, who was facing the wrong way and trimmed the woolly muffler of his grandmother, asleep in the next seat. This fuels speculation that the whiskers are false.

Just My Line

In addition to protesting against the closing of the fine old Hexham-Riccarton railway line – coupled with a tribute to a Mrs. Armfold, whom I promised a mention this week – I want to ask the authorities a question. I shall ask it a few lines further on.

Many times, as I have stood at or near Bellingham Station, awaiting a train, facing roughly in the right direction for getting on it, there has been something I have noticed when the locomotive has drawn up at the platform. Incidentally, the locomotive always does draw up at the platform, one of those abstruse examples of mechanics that stopped me becoming an engine driver. There were several others.

What I have noticed is that the driver and a man on the platform exchange hoops. What is going to happen to those hoops? That is my question. Never say Barras dishonours a promise.

I do not know what those hoops are for, any more than I know what makes the train go. I haven't even worked out yet how I get along myself. (I don't, very well.) I must admit, however, to cherishing a faintly malevolent hope that one day the driver and the man on the platform will miss each other with their hoops, the driver then being obliged to shunt the train backwards so that they can try all over again in reverse.

This is just fantasy, of course. I know that in reality the man on the platform at Bellingham is building a rain butt and the driver, who is fetching the hoops from distant Hawick, keeps bringing the wrong size. One day, the man is going to realise that if you want a thing done properly, you have to do it yourself.

He will have to hurry up, though, if he is not to arrive at the station to find the line forever closed. What is he going to do with all his rain then?

Up North

The Northumbrian Nationalist Movement has been shaken to its core (or gowk). A newly-uncovered spate of manuscripts purports to show that General St. Hubert Fitzpompom DamgudFellah can trace his ancestry back to the legendary Northumbrian kings Wikkabaskit and Splash, that Mr. Leonard Shackleton is entitled to call himself the 94th Earl of Seaburn and that the Thames is a tributary of Willington Gut, joining it at Kirkcudbright.

"Such postulations bode ill for Northumbria," stated the Bishop of Pump and Bucket, when he failed to meet Mr. J.J.T. Backabitt, the Whitley Bay pretender, in No Place yesterday.

Oh!

SIR, – No horse should be made to wear a leather overcoat to distinguish him from a cinema organist. Are there not more obvious differences? In any case, the cinema organist with cold leather next to his skin is able to tell us of his sufferings. Who can say this of the horse?

K.K. GAGGLE, Ponteland.

Or New Ones?

Are you a collector of old masters? Does your wife sample those packets of WHOOSH that are forever being pelted in your door? Do you think these question are superfluous? What about your wife?

Be assured that WHOOSH is not used by art dealers who guarantee to get the muck off your dirty old pictures. On the contrary. Try WHOOSH on your clean old pictures.

Take that picture of a horse in a field in Gateshead painted by your small boy Thomas to your ironmonger. When he has treated it with WHOOSH, it will be as filthy as any old masterpiece. Nothing can be done about this grammar, though.

Why? Why not, if you like? The reason is that WHOOSH contains muck. What about your wife?

It Wouldn't Be

"The Classification of Moths in Relation to the World Distribution of Surplus Financiers." – Arbuthnot Klowte (Buckshee and Zizz, 25s).

This is no book for all who are interested in the economics of multilateral trading exponentiality.

R obert Browning, a compulsive practical joker, used to stuff clergymen's beds with dead birds.

One day, Rossetti said to him, "Have you rooked any good beds lately?"

Browning hit him with A.C. Swinburne, who, as we know, was a small man.

No Offence

"So as not to offend animal lovers, a Wren and a sailor dressed up as a cow."

This selfless example from a military manoeuvre might well be followed on the Durham moors, where sheep-rustling goes on apace. Of course, it would need two small and extremely crafty shepherds to carry the thing off properly. The most inexperienced rustler is going to be suspicious of a sheep which is five feet high and has a ruddy face coming out of a hole in its side.

Two Hexham men named Grupwooth and Spriggminch once dressed up as a bullock for a lark and got themselves knocked down at the market to a short-sighted farmer from Allendale. As they were being driven through Eastgate, Spriggminch, who was the front legs, raised his hat to a Miss Ruby Bawble. A Tom Bogpeece, who was with her, struck the 'bullock' on the flank, eliciting a pained oath from Grupwooth.

At this, a passing animal lover named Bess Toffy struck Bogpeece and was in turn struck by Ruby Bawble. The whole matter was then absurdly complicated by the intervention of two quantity surveyors on a walking tour dressed as a camel for another lark, and a gas inspector dressed as a gas inspector.

"This is ridiculous," the farmer said. "Where is my bullock's hat?"

The matter might not have ended there, but this paragraph does.

Whoa!

Mrs. Blookwith has announced that she will form a Middle-Aged Women's Non-Horse Society if Mr. Phil Thumpable persists in his plan for a tunnel between Longbenton and Backworth. "We keep hearing," she says, "that the tunnel will benefit brewers' horses and old ladies. Some of us in Longbenton and Backworth are neither."

Had she but known, Mr. Thumpable has abandoned his tunnel project, asserting that reformers are always derided, not least if they are derisory. But he has not finished with innovation. He now has plans for the shortest bridge in the world, between his dining room and kitchen.

Of Course

SIR, – In reply to Miss Celia Xenkle, bison have never roamed this country, and neither, I suspect, has Mrs. Laglumb. She and the bison she is alleged to have fallen over are both figments, and gross ones at that.

How can a woman fall over a bison? I once fell over a cow one dark night when I was returning from the annual dinner of the Retired Drapers' Checkers Fellowship, but I ought to have realised that the beast could not negotiate the awkward landing of my first floor flat.

DANIEL WROTTIN, Murton.

Lost

"Always be ready for anything," is a maxim an elderly mentor used to impress upon me. I used belt him gently across the ear.

The trouble with me (Programme up to 1964 – The Troubles With Barras) is that I have devoted so much time to preparing for the disasters which seem likely to descend on me, and none at all to possible multifarious minor mishaps. How many of you – ah, dear readers! – can say that, or would rather have a wholesome bacon sandwich?

Let me, for example, come unexpectedly on an old friend in the street and my wittiest contribution to the conversation that follows will be: "What? Oh, yes," in answer to the question "Well, how are you?"

Other gems from my collection for this occasion are:

1. "Well, well, well!" Spoken with nodding head, the head continuing to nod through the vast pause which follows.
2. "Er – yes, yeees..." Delivered in answer to an unheard question, while gazing unseeingly into the distance.
3. "I see that's a little girl you've got." The child in question is dressed in skirts and has shoulder-length ringlets.
4. "It must be seven years, is it?" This is a theme I hang on to and repeat at 30-second intervals for the rest of the conversation, such as that is.
5. "Well, I have to catch a bus." This after another vast pause during which I have done nothing much more than stand back heavily on the foot of a passer-by.
6. "How's Tom Guppy?" My friend never knew Tom Guppy. I haven't much idea who he is myself.

Still, as I turn away and begin climbing up a telephone box, I have the feeling that in spite of it all, everybody knows what the real Barras is like.

And damned little consolation that is.

More Hints

Mrs. Chump writes: Making a leather bolero for a chest of drawers is really a job for an expert.

It is advisable to get the proportions right from the start, as a chest of drawers with an enormous bolero slopping over it is only slightly less preposterous than a chest of drawers with an obviously too small bolero perched absurdly on top.

Some favour wooden boleros, but these prevent the proper opening of the drawers. Leather boleros are easily torn when the drawers are pulled violently open. If you prefer to remove the bolero before opening the drawers, neither contingency will arise.

Others do not put it on in the first place, but not putting it on in the first place is really a job for an expert.

No Rhyme Here

Regardless of the whereabouts of Pattisbobo, Major Kalamity has decided to sail from Spennymoor Harbour. The decision brings some relief to young Harry Driftwood, who had become half-engaged to Angela Lurchabowte when he half-promised to show her his uncle's yacht, which is a Scotswood sculler. In any case, Angela has become half-engaged to Commander Badstuff, who has three uncles with yachts.

The Admiralty has directed in triplicate that Admiral Shimmering-Dulally's half-pension be donated to the grog fund for aged midshipmen.

Or Dickens?

Next weeks's teaser: 'A horse, a horse!' was spoken by (a) Richard Turpin? (b) Richards (Gordon)? (c) The Bosworth Sisters?

A man went into a hatter's shop and asked for a boot.
"I have no boots, sir," said the hatter. "I can offer you a pair of hats."

Ah, Youth!

There comes to all of us, my friends, a time when we tire of what I call civilisation and long for what I call the call of the wild. It's your call next. I call to mind (my call again) an occasion when dear old Glook and Crumble and I were snowed up in a log cabin in the Canadian sidewoods, just to the right of the backwoods.

"I have travelled the length and breadth of the world..." said Crumble, shooting a look at Glook, who was at the rough deal table, playing patience. I was out of it. I always am when Crumble talks of Life. After all, I myself had travelled the height and circumference, and would have ventured up the hypotenuse if I had found the right angle.

"Well, this is a rough deal and no mistake," said Glook. He shuffled and dealt again.

There was a fearful thumping outside. Glook shuffled again, towards the door, and flung it open. We waited with indrawn breath. Nothing happened, except that we let out our breath again. Outside was only the icy stillness of the primaeval forest.

(PREBENDARY SULPHUR: "I must say you can write these aimless stories as badly as anybody." BARRAS: "Thank you.")

No More?

This week, Professor Beetroot has fallen only once into Mrs. Wibduck's bird bath. Is its power over him waning? If so, what price Dr. Finicky's tests? The doctor asserts that the professor has a high centre of gravity, compensating for his low centre of frivolity. This means that when he leans towards dalliance, always possible in Mrs. Wibduck's presence, he is liable to overbalance.

"This is inconclusive balderdash," states Miss Avril Sleet (née Barras, as aren't they all?).

The professor has promised himself a sabbatical, if he can find one that fits.

Caw!

Bird-watcher-watchers at Glanton are now waiting with stop-watches poised, ready to record which of the bird-watchers rises first to record which of the birds rises first. I forget which bird won last year's early-singing competition, but it is just possible that he climbed back into bed again immediately afterwards, with his head swimming and regretting the whole thing. That is exactly how I felt a few years ago when I tried getting up early (9.30).

I don't know why the Glanton judges judge a bird's rising-time by the hour he begins singing. Some of my friends rise at 6.30, or so they tell me, but they don't sing until around ten. Even then, people discourage them. I myself sometimes fail to sing for days on end, but that doesn't mean I've been asleep all the time. I don't know, though.

And why is it that only the rising-time of the birds excites interest? What about their sleeping habits in general? Which of them sleeps with his knees bent? Does the crow fall over backwards and breathe strangulated bubbles? Is it for this reason that when he gets up he can manage no better song than a hoarse 'caw, caw'?

Finally, have the Glanton experts considered that if they made the bird's life a bit more comfortable, he wouldn't have to get up so early? I know if I had to sleep on dried twigs, I should be up at dawn.

I shouldn't be singing, mind you.

Up North

It is now a matter of some speculation in Northumbrian Nationalist circles whether Cadwatter the ancient Welsh bard ever existed. Recently unearthed documents attributed to him are, not to put too fine a point on it, forgeries. (Forgeries is what they are.)

One such manuscript purports to show that Miss Ella Fitzgerald is Crown Princess to the Northumbrian throne by virtue of her descent from the near-mythical monarch Atisket and his consort Atasket. On the back were the racing results from Gosforth Park.

Is Cadwatter a compositor with the *Wallsend Weekly Buffoon?* The disillusioned Mr. Egbald Knutt is said to have eschewed Northumbrian Nationalism and to be casting about for a fresh, or at least less rancid, heresy.

Contains Muck

Who is this man whose shirt, unfurled,
Shows gleaming white to all the world,
Whose whole demeanour's bright and dapper,
Whose spotless bowler crowns his napper,
Who sports a pair of shining braces

Immune from any filthy traces?
Will no one take aside his wife
And spread the facts of grimy life?
Will no one say, "My dear, your hubby
Can be, like other husbands, grubby!
You'll save your pride a dreadful hurt
By using WHOOSH – it's stuffed with dirt!"

Dark Nights

Mrs. Chump writes: Now is as good a time as any to dismantle an old chair. The wickerwork can be used to make a wickerwork snood for an ironing board. (See my notes on How to Make a Wickerwork Snood for an Ironing Board – 300 guineas, post free.)

Some people favour converting old basket chairs into carpet-sweeper containers, but however expert a job is made of this, the handle of the carpet-sweeper will always tend to stick out. If the handle is detachable, however, it can be wrapped in an old dressing gown and stored separately, or thrown over the fence if you're in a pretty rotten temper.

Never store the sweeping part of the sweeper in this way, as the dressing gown cord is apt to get caught in the works, and you don't want your dressing gown hanging open next time you sweep in mixed company. Although why not?

I forgot to mention in my first sentence that I am still in love with a bashful bachelor, but you don't wish to know that, which is why I bring it up. Why should *you* have all the fun, in mixed company? I also forgot to mention that I was talking about a *basket* chair. You wouldn't get much wickerwork from a non-basket chair, would you? Well, then.

H'm

(PREBENDARY SULPHUR: "What is the point of your first item?" BARRAS: "It has no point. This is art." SULPHUR: "As I thought.")

34

"A chiropodist who moved to first floor premises said at the Bankruptcy Court that what he forgot was that people with bad feet cannot be expected to walk upstairs." – Hitchin Post.

Nor, for that matter, can people with bad feet be expected to travel in a lift if they suffer from claustrophobia. Even if they were free of claustrophobia, suppose they were victims of sticking-out elbows? They could then get comfortably into neither a lift nor a cramped chiropodist's waiting room.

And what is the good of a ground floor consulting room to a chiropodist, if his deaf old housekeeper lives in the attic? I ask this in case he is a chiropodist in a murder mystery. What, for that matter, is the good of a cramped chiropodist? Agility is the thing for a man getting constantly down on his haunches.

Furthermore, if a patient has a bald head as well as bad feet, he is going to be pretty uncomfortable sitting in the waiting room, if there is a small boy with bad feet also sitting there making unpleasant remarks about his bald head. And if the patient is short-sighted as well as bad-footed (and bald), no matter where the consulting room is, he will stand on all the other patients' feet on the way in.

Easily the best plan for the anxious chiropodist is to take a postal course in carpentry or short story writing. He can then save up his chiropody for his spare time, practising on his stronger friends.

The postman will not mind where he lives. Unless he has bad feet.

What Bison?

SIR, – The history of Mrs. Laglumb and the bison has become somewhat distorted over the years, and so has Mrs. Laglumb. The truth is that she did not fall over the bison, but off it, a much more plausible contingency.

The beast sat down suddenly in Abomination Street, Prudhoe, and Mrs. Laglumb slid off behind. In a way, this was a milestone in Prudhoe's battered history, as it was the first time a Mrs. Veronica Laglumb had fallen off a bison there, although a Mrs. Winnie Laglumb did so in 1872.

EVANGELINE VUMP, Stannington.

Knees Sense

Miss Gwendoline Goggling's appointment as Bedlington's or Gateshead's Vital Statistic Queen has still not gone unopposed in Gateshead or Bedlington. Miss Nottarf is now protesting that three of the five Jarrow judges were biased in favour of northern knee beauty.

"I am a Darlington girl," she states. "My knees are exotically southern in their beauty."

Miss Nottarf's vital statistic is 13 inches. It is well known that in Jarrow a 13-inch knee is considered somewhat over-voluptuous.

"Gateshead is as good as Bedlington to a blind horse," is the legal advice of Mr. Gilliefeather Hoote, Q.C., which will cost somebody dear.

So Do I

The romance of international geophysics is something which is hardly appreciated by the man in the street. Mostly he is thinking about the woman in the next street. Indeed it can fairly be said that a question the man in the street seldom asks himself is: What is international geophysics and where can I get some? This is what the International Geophysical Year, which begins its run next July (booking now open), ought to take into account.

I have nothing against international geophysicists. Perhaps their ears are a bit big, but I am sure they have their reasons. This column has a long history of tolerance (a fortnight). But it is no good their thinking that all this observation of the earth's magnetism, or the aurora, or the ionosphere, is going to win back the missing millions to clippie mat-making.

Let us face it. What the public wants is titillation. I am not denying that this is regrettable. I am not even saying I regret it. But there it is. (No, there!) International geophysics *qua* international geophysics is a dead letter. But international geophysics plus titillation! That could well be the biggest thing since the epidiascope.

It is, however, an idle hope. International geophysicists live in a dream world of their own. They have just put out the announcement that their International Geophysical Year is to last from July 1957 until December 1958. Well, really! Who will heed their prognostications after that? If they truly believe that July 1957 to December 1958 adds up to a year, they will believe anything.

All I can say is that for many of us reading that announcement, the ionosphere will never be the same again.

Farewell

Shall we hear again from the ketch Imbendin? She has sailed once more from Spennymoor Harbour. There was little ceremony.

"What point was there in elaborate goodbyes?" asked Councillor Mrs. Wallop. "They may well be back on the next tide."

We shall see. Skipper Joe Weskit has set a course for Iceland by way of the South Pacific. He is fairly sure Pattisbobo is in one of these two regions. Will he recognise it if he sees it? "All islands have one thing in common," he informed young Harry Driftwood. "So Admiral Collingwood told me. Not that he said what it was."

Major Kalamity is entirely confident. He reassures himself that Livingstone found Lake Victoria when he was looking for his binoculars.

J.H. Again

Soak your socks in WHOOSH while you are asleep (a devilish difficult thing to do) and at 5 p.m. next day your calves will drop off.

"It was on father's knee that I first discovered WHOOSH," writes Mr. J.H., of Hebburn (obscurely). "It had to be father's knee, as there was only water on mother's."

Still Around

Omniscient Thurlow Oxxe writes: The necessity to re-orient public utility combined enterprises constitutes a basic countervailing power to the non-wealth-producing consumer. Cartel interventions notwithstanding, corporations will concentrate bullishly while exchange mechanisms fluctuate. Streets will get wet if it rains.

"A bowler hat is more authoritative. We don't want people to confuse our meter-readers with bus drivers, guards and postmen." – The Gas Board, speaking for England.

Stationmasters, on the other hand, wear bowler hats to deter women from asking whether the train destined for York is going there. Dignity has nothing to do with it. It was Burns, I believe (it wasn't Allen), who said: "The rank is but the guinea stamp" – a splendid sentiment which I sometimes mull over and leave where it is.

Bus drivers wear leather overcoats in order not to be confused with theodolite gaugers, cinema organists and horses. Guards wear squeaky boots in order not to be confused with other guards, whether fire or security. Coastguards wear squeaky boots to stamp on women who ask what makes the sea grey in Scarborough. Postmen every now and then dash about on all fours shouting "Dweeeee!" just for the hell of it, or to get into this farrago.

Of course, the gasman beneath the bowler is nearly all human. He may strike a chill as he steps across the threshold with a terse "Gas!" but the authoritarian mask disguises a shy romantic creature. He harbours thoughts of a great love, but until the lady cinema organist or theodolite gauger of his dreams comes along he will make do with gas and patting horses.

I myself (old Barras in person) have known a gasman so far lose his iron aplomb as to fling open a wrong cupboard and be showered with pans and broomsticks. A bowler hat, you may think, sits ill on that kind of thing. But if the essential man is decent and honourable, what boots it? Or even what squeaky boots it?

Teaser XUF/47

For a total of 59s. 6d., a man buys a disused cow, three marlin spike containers, two papier mâché door-knobs, a green leather hatstand, 27 photographs of Jarrow and a bottle.

Why?

Now, Miss Vump

SIR, – I have studied the bison in more than one of its vicissitudes. Miss Evangeline Vump states that Mrs. Laglumb's bison sat down in Prudhoe. No! It will not stand up to cold scrutiny!

The bison sinking to rest invariably sticks its head between its knees, utters a long-drawn "Aaaah," like a man lowering himself into a cold bath, and puts down its forelegs first. In no circumstances could Mrs. Laglumb have slipped off the rear end of the beast, unless she was indulging in some unseemly antics. Was it not a tapir?

Tapirs are sometimes given to frolicking. I have watched bison for 27 years – and sometimes caught them watching me – and they are decorous creatures.

U.U. EEJᴧH, Mickley.

Shame!

"Quick blowing zephyrs vex daft Jim."

Into these impetuous words, Mr. J.C.F., of Newcastle, claims to have compressed the 26 letters of the alphabet – though, as I understand it, his hat fell off near the finish.

Now I have no quarrel with Mr. F. I think I once met his uncle in Carlisle; I can't be sure, as I have met a few uncles there. It is not the technical brilliance of the feat that saddens me, but rather the sentiment involved.

If the Jim in question is Jim Claggersby, of Seaton Delaval, as I believe is the case, then I feel that Mr. F. is being less than fair. (If he is not Jim Claggersby, but some other Jim, I withdraw unreservedly and there is no point in my going on. I am going on.)

No one would deny that Jim Claggersby has been known to get sulky in a high wind, but those of us who know him best know that there is good reason for this. He has water on his right knee. Nor is it a fact that a mere zephyr would upset him. He has an elastic knee-band which I lent him in 1951. Nothing, I feel, less than a near-gale would huff him now. I also feel that I have not much chance of getting my elastic knee-band back.

As for the description of Jim Claggersby as 'daft Jim', this is going too far. It is true that he wears his shirts upside-down and hee-haws like a donkey, but apart from this his only eccentricity is to climb drainpipes in the nude.

No. If I had the re-writing of that sentence, I should amend it thus: "Strong winds amounting to near gale force have been known, because of his knee infirmity, to cause some irritation to mildly idiosyncratic Jim Claggersby."

I do not claim that this contains all the letters of the alphabet, but at least it has some regard for veracity. Let us have fair play, Mr. F.

Yes

There is always some heartening intelligence. "Sanitary engineers will now be known as health inspectors," I read.

Dan, Dan, the sanitary man,
Declines any more to carry the can;
If the smell on the landing becomes much intenser,
Send for Daniel, Daniel, the hygiene dispenser.

Aspiration

Constantly, except for 16 hours a day, tests are being carried out on WHOOSH (with an 'h'), by scientists who are paid (good) money. It was in 1903 that Dr. Yubblitt pointed out that if it were not for the impurities in alcohol it would be a killer. It might have been 1904, unless that was the year he pointed out that Dr. Klatter had stolen his pipette.

"Pure alcohol is poison," said Dr. Yubblitt, and he was the lad to know.

So it is with WHOOSH (with an 'h'). Pure WHOOSH would rot a man's athletic trunks at 50 feet. But WHOOSH contains muck! – and the daintiest of athletic trunks can be submitted to its filthy touch. WHOOSH!

Envoi

You must have guessed, my friends, that it would happen. Yesterday I received a call from my old chief, Sir Hugo Ivebeen of M.I.5., and have sailed off on a noxious enterprise (with two funnels, you may wager).

I am leaving this column, all ends untied, in the hands of old Mother Mawkish, the editor's niece, and God bless nepotism! She will find both of the jokes at the back of the drawer.